A Student's Guide
to Goethe

D1614393

STUDENTS' GUIDES TO EUROPEAN LITERATURE

General Editor: Brian Masters

A Student's Guide to Goethe

by

F. J. LAMPORT

Fellow of Worcester College, Oxford

HEINEMANN EDUCATIONAL BOOKS

LONDON

Heinemann Educational Books Ltd
22 Bedford Square, London WC1B 3HH

LONDON EDINBURGH MELBOURNE AUCKLAND
HONG KONG SINGAPORE KUALA LUMPUR NEW DELHI
IBADAN NAIROBI JOHANNESBURG KINGSTON
EXETER (NH)   PORT OF SPAIN

ISBN 0 435 37572 5

Printed in Great Britain by Spottiswoode Ballantyne Ltd.
Colchester and London

Contents

Foreword

This book is intended to be, as its title says, a guide. That is, it aims not to express, still less convert the reader to, any particular point of view, but to suggest how the student making Goethe's acquaintance for the first time may best approach his major works and form critical opinions of his own. A work of this size cannot be exhaustive or anything approaching it, and I hope the student will realize this. Often discussion and illustration have had to be cursory. Where I have dwelt on detail I have been trying to show the reader the *kind* of thing he should be looking for. I have tried to indicate those features of Goethe's works which seem to me particularly characteristic of their author or of a certain phase of his creative career. Here my selection and presentation of material may well reveal my own especial interests or prejudices, but I have aimed at objectivity throughout. I have also tried to point to major areas of critical disagreement, topics on which the student should be made aware of controversy and encouraged to work out his own point of view.

Quotations are from the 'Hamburger Ausgabe' (*HA*) of Goethe's works (see Bibliography, p. 121), in which spelling and punctuation are modernized. References are however given by title and chapter, scene, etc., so that quotations may be easily located in any edition. The translations are my own, and are strictly working cribs. That is, they are deliberately literal rather than literary, and intended to help the student understand the original, not to be a substitute for it.

Many ideas which have found direct or indirect expression in this book have arisen in discussion with colleagues and with pupils to whom I owe a general debt of gratitude. I should also like to thank the General Editor of this series for his encouragement and patience.   F.J.L.

1

Introduction

Critical approaches

There are many ways of approaching an author and his work. The 'positivist' nineteenth century was largely interested in facts, and collected these in a manner which to later generations has often seemed unselective and uncritical; this does not mean, however, that facts are quite unimportant. This method of study was largely superseded, in the later part of the nineteenth century and the early years of our own, by attempts to form pictures of the 'essence' of an author, syntheses of his life and works from some particular interpretative, often philosophical or even ideological, point of view. The danger of this is of course that factual details which do not fit the grand design may be glossed over or suppressed. Most modern criticism, at any rate in the West, tends to concentrate on the literary work itself, on poetic forms and structures. Here the danger is that the work may come to be seen in a vacuum, and if this happens then the Marxist reproach of 'formalism' will be justified.

Goethe's remark in his autobiography *Dichtung und Wahrheit* that his works were all 'Bruchstücke einer grossen Konfession' ('fragments of a great confession') has all too often been taken as an excuse for biographical source-grubbing, particularly where his numerous love-affairs are concerned. Goethe himself mocks the 'anecdote-hunters' in the poem *Geheimstes* (*Most Secret*) in the *West-östlicher Divan*:

„Wir sind emsig, nachzuspüren,
Wir, die Anekdotenjäger,
Wer dein Liebchen sei und ob du
Nicht auch habest viele Schwäger.

Denn dass du verliebt bist, sehn wir,
Mögen es dir gerne gönnen;
Doch dass Liebchen so dich liebe,
Werden wir nicht glauben können."

Ungehindert, liebe Herren,
Sucht sie auf! nur hört das Eine:
Ihr erschrecket, wenn sie dasteht!
Ist sie fort, ihr kost dem Scheine.

'We are busy tracking down, we, the anecdote-hunters, who your
lady-love is and whether you haven't got a lot of brothers-in-law. For
we can see that you are in love, and we don't want to spoil it; but that
your lady-love loves you so, we can't believe.'—Don't let me stop you,
gentlemen, find her out! but let me tell you one thing: you will have a
shock when she stands before you! When she is gone, you can love
the illusion. (ll. 1–12)

Research continues to reveal more and more facts hitherto
unknown or unsuspected—such as, ironically enough, the
identity of the lady referred to in this very poem. But most
modern critics would agree that what matters to the reader of
Goethe's works is not to identify their raw material but to see
what Goethe has made of it and how. A work such as Barker
Fairley's *A Study of Goethe* shows the value of biographical
data and of an analysis of personality in an appreciation of
Goethe the creative artist, healing what Fairley describes as
'the rift in Goethe criticism which tends to take his biographers
in one direction and his interpreters in another'.

Just as different ages prefer different methods of literary
study, so too they have different tastes. A comparison of
selections of Goethe's poetry published at different times will
show a growing taste for the poems of his old age as against
those of his youth and early manhood, which formerly enjoyed
the greater esteem. In a body of work as large as Goethe's,
produced over an exceptionally long creative life, there will
clearly be great variety. Different ages will find themselves
attracted by different things, and they will develop new theories

and methods of criticism to account for their tastes; then in turn they will tend to prefer the kind of works which most usefully illustrate the validity of their new critical theories and methods. The theories of symbolism, and the modern taste for the ambiguous and fragmentary, for what is suggestive of a multiplicity of meanings rather than simple and easily categorized, have led to an increasing appreciation of the works of Goethe's old age, such as *Wilhelm Meisters Wanderjahre* and the Second Part of *Faust*. Thus whereas G. H. Lewes in his *Life and Works of Goethe* (1855) described the fragmentary character of *Nicht zu weit* (one of the interpolated short stories in the *Wanderjahre*) as 'an impertinence to the public', a modern editor (Erich Trunz in the 'Hamburger Ausgabe') writes that it is deliberately fragmentary because it is tragic and the problems it portrays are insoluble. A modern critic is similarly unlikely to echo Lewes's verdict that *Faust II* is 'an elaborate mistake'. It is generally a good critical principle to assume that artists know what they are doing, and to adopt an interpretative approach designed to bring out the merits rather than the demerits of their works. Some modern Goethe criticism, however, might perhaps benefit from a little scepticism. Goethe's treatment of form is often problematic, sometimes casual, and some critics appear over-zealous in their hunt for subtleties and profundities.

One modern school of criticism in particular is resolutely opposed to an aesthetic view of the work of art in isolation and purely for its own sake. This is, of course, the Marxist school, which sees the validity and significance of a work of art in its reflexion (or, in the case of what is by this criterion an inferior work, its evasion) of economic and socio-political reality. The most prominent Marxist critic of Goethe is Georg Lukács, who sees, for instance, Mephistopheles in *Faust* as an image of the spirit of capitalism. Such ideas as these may often seem forced, and the Marxist, like any critic seeking to demonstrate a particular thesis, is all too likely to distort or suppress uncomfortable facts. But he may also suggest to us new and fruitful ways of looking at seemingly familiar works, and perform a valuable service in reminding us that no artist lives, and no work of art is produced, in a vacuum, but that they inevitably reflect the characteristics of their historical period.

Biography

Johann Wolfgang Goethe was born on 28 August 1749 at Frankfurt-am-Main, at that time a Free City of the Holy Roman Empire—in effect a tiny self-contained republic. His parents were well-to-do middle-class people; not, as is sometimes said, 'patrician', though his father had purchased a sinecure which carried the title 'Rat' ('Counsellor'). His mother was by far the more powerful personality of the two, very much a character in her own right; like her famous son she attained a high old age (eighteen when he was born, she lived to be seventy-seven) and her letters are a fascinating mirror of the times. Only one other of her children survived infancy: the second, Cornelia, born in December 1750.

The young Goethe was sent to the University of Leipzig in 1765 to study law. He remained in Leipzig until 1768, when he returned home to Frankfurt suffering from a never-identified, possibly psychosomatic illness. He resumed his legal studies in Strasbourg in 1770, but did not succeed in obtaining his doctorate. Here, however, under the catalytic influence of J. G. Herder (1744–1803), one of the most influential German thinkers of the century, he found his own creative self. Of his youthful emotional attachments the most serious were that with Friederike Brion (1770–1), which produced some of his first distinctive lyric poetry, that with Lotte Buff (1772), which was one of the originating experiences for *Werther*, and that with Lili Schönemann, to whom he became engaged in April 1775.

In September 1775 he was invited to Weimar, in Saxony: the

capital of one of the many minute principalities which, together
with the larger states such as Prussia and Austria, and the Free
Cities like his birthplace, Frankfurt, went to make up the loose
confederacy of the Empire. He was to be the companion of the
young Duke, Karl August, who, born in 1757, had just attained
his majority and taken over the reins of government from his
mother, the Dowager Duchess Anna Amalia. Goethe undertook
a number of administrative duties, became a member of the
Duke's Privy Council ('Geheimer Rat') in 1779, and in 1782
received the patent of nobility, entitling him to the style '*von*
Goethe'. These years in Weimar were also the years of an
intimate, though almost certainly platonic, relationship with
Charlotte von Stein, the unhappy wife of a Weimar court
nobleman.

In 1786 Goethe felt an irresistible desire to escape from
Weimar, and without telling anyone of his intentions went off
to Italy. He stayed away from Weimar for almost two years;
but on his return he remained there for the rest of his life without further major interruptions, his longest period of absence
being a journey to the valleys of the Rhine and Main in 1815.
At his own request, he was officially relieved of his govern-
mental duties, but he took an increasing part in directing cultural affairs. He also found himself a permanent partner,
Christiane Vulpius, though he did not formally marry her
until October 1806 (their son August, then approaching seventeen, was one of the witnesses). This liaison did not prevent other
love-affairs, one in particular (with Marianne von Willemer in
1814–15) productive of some of his finest poetry. Also of vital
importance in Goethe's creative life was his friendship and
collaboration with Friedrich Schiller. This literary partnership,
which marks the years of 'Weimar classicism' at its height,
lasted from July 1794 until the death of Schiller in May 1805.

Now, one by one, the other figures died who had played their
parts in his life: in 1808 his mother, in 1816 his wife Christiane,
in 1827 Charlotte von Stein; in 1828 Karl August, elevated

by the Congress of Vienna in 1815 to the rank of Grand Duke, and in 1830 Goethe's only son, named August after his patron. In 1821 began the last of Goethe's major emotional attachments, to the seventeen-year-old Ulrike von Levetzow: his proposal of marriage to her was declined, but once again the encounter bore fruit in magnificent poetry. In 1831 Goethe at last put the finishing touches to *Faust*, his life's work, which had occupied him on and off since the early 1770's; on 22 March 1832 he died, in his eighty-third year. An almost exact English contemporary was the Radical and Utilitarian philosopher Jeremy Bentham (1748–1832)—whom Goethe referred to, in a conversation with Eckermann on 17 March 1829, as 'that old radical fool'.

Johann Peter Eckermann (1792–1854) was Goethe's literary assistant from 1823 onwards, and one of his closest associates in the last years of his life. Eckermann's record of his *Conversations with Goethe* is a classic in its own right. Nietzsche declared it to be the best book in the German language; it has also been described as Goethe's own last masterpiece.

The historical background

Goethe's long life began in surroundings which were in many respects still medieval, and ended in the days of the first railways, of plans for the Suez and Panama Canals and of increasing industrialization. He was well aware of these radical changes in the economic basis of existence and the changes in the quality of life which they were already bringing about. In the political sphere, Goethe witnessed the French Revolution of 1789 and himself accompanied the Duke of Weimar, who was a commander in the Prussian army, on the counter-revolutionary campaign launched against France by Austria and Prussia in 1792. He saw the rise and fall of Napoleon—whom he met personally in 1808—and the period of reaction which followed the Vienna Congress of 1815. He saw the restoration of the

French monarchy, and the replacement of the reactionary
Charles X by the 'citizen king' Louis-Philippe as a result of
the July Revolution of 1830, which marked the beginnings of a
new phase of democratic revolution. Goethe himself was little
interested in politics, although he viewed democratic move-
ments, and all violent forms of social and political change, with
disfavour.

> Das liebe, heil'ge röm'sche Reich,
> Was hält's nur noch zusammen?

The dear old Holy Roman Empire, what still keeps it together?

—sing the students in the 'Auerbachs Keller' scene of *Faust*. By
the time the first part of *Faust* was completed, the Holy Roman
Empire was indeed no more; but under the German Con-
federation established at the Congress of Vienna, the small
principalities, such as Weimar, went on very much as they had
done before the Napoleonic upheavals, and the struggle for
hegemony between Austria and Prussia, which was to lead
under Bismarck to the creation of a politically united Germany,
had hardly begun in Goethe's lifetime. In such circumstances
as these, the indifference of Goethe—like so many German
writers—to political affairs is not surprising. Yet here too
Goethe was aware that after all the old Europe had gone and
could not return. At the cannonade of Valmy in September
1792, which marked the turning-point of the counter-
revolutionary campaign, he declared—according to his later
account in the *Campagne in Frankreich*—

> Von hier und heute geht eine neue Epoche der Welt-
> geschichte aus, und ihr könnt sagen, ihr seid dabei gewesen.

Here and now a new epoch of world history is beginning, and you will
be able to say you were there when it happened. (*Campagne in Frankreich*, entry for 19 September 1792)

The philosophical background

The years of Goethe's manhood were also the years in which the greatest of German philosophers, Immanuel Kant (1724–1804), published his major works, beginning with the *Kritik der reinen Vernunft* (*Critique of Pure Reason*) in 1781. In his old age Goethe claimed that Kant had influenced him, but he was not a philosopher: the intellectual discipline of philosophy he found too rigorous. He did not spend years wrestling with Kantian doctrine, as Schiller did. The Kantian distinction between appearance and reality, so important for Kleist and the Romantics, finds as such no echo in his work—though he was led on his own way to the similar conclusion that

> Alles Vergängliche
> Ist nur ein Gleichnis
>
> Everything transient is only a parable. (*Faust II*, closing scene)

He rejected Kant's doctrine of radical evil, seeing the world as ultimately and essentially harmonious (which does not, however, preclude individual tragedy). For a similar reason he rejected Christianity, with its stress, as he saw it, on sin and suffering. He was at times outspokenly anti-Christian, and remains non-Christian even when—as in the closing scenes of *Faust II* or *Die Wahlverwandtschaften*—he makes use of Christian imagery. The modern philosophers whose influence is most readily traceable in his work are Leibniz and Spinoza. Leibniz (1646–1716) had taught that the universe is made up of a multiplicity of dynamic units or spiritual atoms, which he called *monads*. Spinoza (1632–77) was only in Goethe's lifetime beginning to be respected, after having long been condemned as a dangerous atheist; in fact he had taught, though in a very austere form, the 'pantheist' doctrine that nature and God are one.

Scientific thought also plays an important part in Goethe's view of the universe. The seventeenth century had been dominated by the great mathematicians, Descartes and Leibniz, and the earlier part of the eighteenth century by the great physicist, Newton; Goethe's lifetime saw the beginnings of modern chemistry and of the biological sciences. Goethe himself was greatly interested in scientific work, particularly in geology, biology, and optics. In the second of these he made a number of valuable contributions. He was one of the first to demonstrate the existence in man of an intermaxillary bone, the bone holding the incisor teeth. This discovery was regarded as of great importance at the time, for it was evidence of continuity between man and the lower orders of creation. Goethe was also the founder of a new discipline in the biological sciences, comparative morphology. In optics he himself was convinced that he had made an even more important discovery. This was his theory of light and colours, with which he claimed to have proved Newton wrong, and which he regarded as his greatest achievement—more important by far than his poetry. The verdict of posterity has been very different. Yet an important part of the image of Goethe is that of the *uomo universale* or Universal Man, like those of the Italian renaissance: poet, statesman, scientist and sage. It is important to remember that the different branches of knowledge were not in Goethe's day so specialized, nor the sheer quantity of knowledge so great, as to prevent a gifted amateur from attaining a considerable understanding of a number of subjects. Goethe's scientific work is also of general importance to the student of his works for the attitude to nature and to knowledge which it reveals.

The literary background

Modern German literature begins in the age of Goethe. During his early years, Klopstock (born in 1724) in lyric poetry, Lessing (born in 1729) in the drama, and Wieland (born in 1733) in the novel, were beginning to lay the foundations. But

the mid-eighteenth century was a period of uncertainty. Each
of the three writers mentioned, for example, was in his own
way conscious of a need for new literary forms to express new
subject-matter and new sensibilities. This phenomenon has
been interpreted in terms of the awakening of the middle
classes and the end of the cultural domination of the aristocracy; or of the awakening of individualism, the discovery of
every man's right—in the words of the American Declaration
of Independence, a characteristic document of the 1770's—to
'life, liberty and the pursuit of happiness', and to an individual
self-expression for which the rigid conventional forms of
earlier literature could not provide. At all events, there was no
established tradition of long standing when Goethe's first
works appeared. Indeed many of the traditions of German
literature were founded by him: that of the historical drama
with *Götz von Berlichingen*, that of the 'Bildungsroman' with
Wilhelm Meisters Lehrjahre. And since there were no recognized models, his works not only could be, but had to be,
experimental: in all genres he created his own forms.

Periods of Goethe's life

Goethe's work before 1770 is largely conventional, and hardly
warrants regarding as a separate period. He himself considered
the Italian journey of 1786 as the major turning-point of his
creative life, and the period up to this date, comprising the
years of his youth and early manhood, may be taken as a unit.
But he was already thirty-seven when he went to Italy, and
in fact 1775, the year in which he moved to Weimar, makes a
suitable division between his early 'Storm and Stress' years and
those in which he was already moving towards a more 'classical' style. His classical period proper begins with the Italian
journey and lasts through the years of collaboration with
Schiller; about the turn of the century begins the final phase,
in which he moves away from classicism to the fragmentary,

symbolist style of his last works. In this book I have accordingly adopted the following fourfold division:

1 Rococo and 'Sturm und Drang' ('Storm and Stress'): up to 1775
2 First Weimar period: 1775–1786
3 The Classical Goethe: 1786–1806
4 The Later Years: 1806–1832

Obviously there will be some overlap between the phases of any such rough division. *Faust* spans all four periods—the First Part contains elements which date back to the early 1770s, but was not completed till 1806; the Second Part was concluded in 1831. The *Wilhelm Meister* novels similarly occupy a wide span of Goethe's creative life, but in fact the *Lehrjahre* and *Wanderjahre* do each belong to a separate phase. More difficult are the cases of *Egmont*, which dates in inspiration from the 'Sturm und Drang' phase, but was only completed in Italy, and *Iphigenie* and *Tasso*, which similarly date from the first Weimar period but had to wait till the classical period for completion. I have chosen here to discuss each of these three plays in the context of the period to which its conception belongs. *Faust* might seem all the more to warrant this treatment in that the unity of the finished work is highly problematic. Precisely for this reason, however, the process of completion and the respective final shape of the completed two parts must be regarded as of the highest importance. Moreover, not only the solutions, but the nature and extent of the problems involved seem only to have become clear to Goethe in the course of working; and Part I and Part II seem fittingly to conclude the classical and final periods of his life respectively.

2

Rococo and 'Sturm und Drang': up to 1775

A. General characterization

1. Rococo
The term 'rococo' is originally an architectural one, derived from *rocaille*, a kind of frothy decoration in stucco, frequently seen in eighteenth-century churches and palaces, particularly in France and Southern Germany. In literature the term denotes a formal, decorative, conventional style, which aims to entertain rather than to express any particular personal experience or feeling. Much lyrical poetry was written in the *anacreontic* manner (supposedly in imitation of the Greek poet Anacreon), singing the pleasures of wine and love with elegant frivolity and often with carefully controlled innuendo. The young Goethe wrote a number of poems in this conventional manner, and two plays which also conform to established eighteenth-century types: *Die Laune des Verliebten* (*A Lover's Moods*, 1765), which is a 'Schäferspiel' or pastoral—that is, a play featuring enamoured shepherds and shepherdesses in an idyllic pseudo-Greek setting; and *Die Mitschuldigen* (*The Accomplices*, 1768), a farce, with a vaguely modern setting but with the characters bearing a mixture of native names (Söller, Sophie) and classical (Alceste). This is common in 'classical' comedy (cf. Molière). Both these plays are written in *alexandrines*, the conventional 'classical' dramatic verse taken over by the Germans from France.

2. *'Sturm und Drang'*

This curious phrase is literally translated 'Storm and Stress', but idiomatically it means something like 'untamed youth' or 'sowing one's wild oats'. It is the title of a wild and woolly play published in 1776 by F. M. Klinger; and from this source it has been adopted by literary historians to denote the epoch of German literature lasting approximately from 1767 into the mid-eighties.

(*a*) *'Genie' and 'Kraft'*. The epoch is also called the 'Geniezeit' (age of genius), since one of its major characteristic features is the emphasis placed upon the free expression of creative genius, as opposed to the conventions and rules which the writer had been expected to observe hitherto (e.g. the dramatic 'rule' of the Three Unities, as in the classical French theatre). The 'Stürmer und Dränger', the adherents of this brief movement, were themselves sometimes—ironically—referred to as 'Genies' or 'Kraftgenies'. They admired 'Kraft' (power, vigour, force, energy), both in poetic language and expression and as embodied in the 'Kraftkerl' or 'Kraftmensch', the powerful, self-reliant individual. In Goethe's dramatic sketch *Götter, Helden, und Wieland* (*Gods, Heroes, and Wieland*)—a burlesque of the emasculated treatment, as Goethe saw it, of classical mythology in Wieland's *Alceste*—we meet such a 'Kerl' in the person of Hercules, who gives a definition of the type which we may quote as characteristic, despite its exaggerated, parodistic tone:

WIELAND: Was nennt ihr brave Kerls?

HERKULES: Einen, der mitteilt, was er hat. Und der reichste ist der bravste. Hatte einer Überfluss an Kräften, so prügelte er die andern aus. Und versteht sich, ein rechter Mann gibt sich nie mit Geringern ab, nur mit seinesgleichen, auch Grössern wohl. Hatte einer denn Überfluss an Säften, machte er den Weibern so viel Kinder, als sie begehrten, auch wohl ungebeten. Wie ich denn selbst in einer Nacht funfzig Buben ausgearbeitet habe. Fehlt es einem denn an beiden, und der Himmel hatte ihm, oder auch wohl dazu, Erb und Hab vor Tausenden gegeben, eröffnete er seine Türen und hiess Tausende willkommen, mit ihm zu geniessen. . . .

WIELAND: Das meiste davon wird zu unsern Zeiten für Laster gerechnet.

WIELAND: What do you mean, fine fellows? HERCULES: One who gives out what he's got. And the richest is the finest. If one had too much strength then he'd give the others a thrashing. And of course, a real man won't bother himself with anyone smaller than he is, only with his equals, or bigger men too. And if one had too much juice, then he'd give the women as many children as they wanted, without their asking too. As I once got fifty boys in a single night myself. But if a man had neither, and heaven had given him instead or, come to that, as well, more wealth and goods than thousands of others, he'd open his doors and welcome thousands in to enjoy it with him . . .

WIELAND: Most of that is nowadays accounted vice.

(b) *Nature.* 'Natur' was another of the battle-cries of the 'Stürmer und Dränger'. They echoed Rousseau's demand for man to return to nature, and admired 'natural' manners, feelings and modes of expression uncorrupted by civilized effeteness. They experienced external nature—rivers and hills, forests and fields and trees—with a new immediacy and intensity, as the source of 'Kraft', of energy and life. Goethe makes Egmont, in his prison soliloquy in Act V, speak of drawing refreshment from nature after being confined in the council chamber. Faust longs for contact with nature:

Wo fass' ich dich, unendliche Natur?
Euch Brüste, wo? Ihr Quellen alles Lebens—

Where may I catch hold of you, infinite nature? You breasts, where? You sources of all life—(*Faust*, ll. 455-6)

But Werther comes to the awesome realization that Nature does not only create, but also destroys what she has created.

> ... mir untergräbt das Herz die verzehrende Kraft, die in dem All der Natur verborgen liegt; die nichts gebildet hat, das nicht seinen Nachbar, nicht sich selbst zerstörte. Und so taumle ich beängstigt. Himmel und Erde und ihre webenden Kräfte um mich her: ich sehe nichts als ein ewig verschlingendes, ewig wiederkäuendes Ungeheuer.

> ... my heart is undermined by the consuming force that lies concealed in the totality of nature; that has created nothing which does not destroy its neighbour and itself. And so I reel in terror. Heaven and earth and their weaving forces all about me: I see nothing but an ever-swallowing, ever-regurgitating monster. (*Werther*, Book I, letter of 18 August)

(c) *Herder*. Johann Gottfried Herder (1744–1803) was the major theorist of the movement. In his writings he stressed the importance of national character in art and the expressive power of primitive, unsophisticated poetry. Goethe came under his influence in Strasbourg in 1770: Herder had come to Strasbourg for a course of operations for his eyesight, Goethe to resume his legal studies which had been interrupted in 1768. But Herder awakened Goethe's creative personality: his theories of national character and natural modes of expression were a revelation to the younger man. In 1773 Herder published a kind of manifesto he had edited, entitled *Von Deutscher Art und Kunst* (*German Character and German Art*). One of the contributions was an essay by Goethe on Gothic (or, as he calls it, 'German') architecture. Goethe sees the cathedral of Strasbourg in the light of Herder's theories as expressing the German spirit, and thus superior to the 'foreign' classical manner which had prevailed for centuries in various modifications (Renaissance, Baroque and Rococo). The most important essays in the manifesto are, however, two by Herder himself, on subjects in which he had exerted the most crucial influence on Goethe. One is on Shakespeare; the other on Ossian and folk poetry. (Ossian was alleged author of certain largely bogus primitive Gaelic epics, whose 'discovery' and publication by James Macpherson in the 1760s was one of the major literary sensations of the eighteenth century.) In the Shakespeare essay Herder praises the Englishman's plays and his freedom from the restraints of the French theatre as the natural dramatic expression of the Nordic spirit. Herder's view of Shakespeare bore fruit in Goethe's first major play, *Götz von Berlichingen*, and its influence can still be felt in *Egmont*. Following in Herder's wake, Goethe himself wrote an essay on Shakespeare (*Rede zum Shakespeares-Tag*) in which Shakespeare's works are praised in typical 'Sturm und Drang' fashion as embodying and expressing 'Natur! Natur!' Ossian too Herder sees as a typical representative of the Nordic spirit—for the Germans enthusiastically confused Germanic and Celtic prehistory and myth. He is also the purveyor of a characteristic kind of romantic melancholy and gloom which is echoed in *Werther*: the final climax of Goethe's novel is actually marked by a lengthy reading from Ossian. Herder praises folk poetry for its directness and 'dramatic' quality, and this theory is also reflected in Goethe's plays, as well as in the lyric poetry he wrote at this time, some of it in direct imitation of the folk-ballad style.

B. Poetry

1. Poetry of experience: the lyric and ballad

Goethe had his eyes opened by Herder to the expressive, as opposed to the merely decorative, possibilities of poetry, of which there are only occasional intimations in his earlier verse. Now he began to express personal feelings and personal experience, of nature and of love. The poems written for Friederike Brion, the pastor's daughter of Sesenheim, near Strasbourg, mark the transition. Thus a poem like *Mit einem gemalten Band* (*With a Painted Ribbon*) is still in many ways Rococo:

Kleine Blumen, kleine Blätter
Streuen mir mit leichter Hand
Gute junge Frühlingsgötter
Tändelnd auf ein luftig Band.

Zephyr, nimm's auf deine Flügel,
Schling's um meiner Liebsten Kleid!
Und so tritt sie vor den Spiegel
All in ihrer Munterkeit.

Sieht mit Rosen sich umgeben,
Selbst wie eine Rose jung:
Einen Blick, geliebtes Leben!
Und ich bin belohnt genung.

Fühle, was dies Herz empfindet,
Reiche frei mir deine Hand,
Und das Band, das uns verbindet,
Sei kein schwaches Rosenband!

Little flowers, little leaves, kindly young gods of spring strew for me with light and playful touch on an airy ribbon. Zephyr, bear it on your wings, wind it about my love's dress! And so she steps before the mirror in all her gaiety. Sees herself surrounded with roses, herself youthful as a rose: One look, beloved creature! and I am rewarded enough. Feel what this heart is feeling, freely give me your hand, and let the bond that joins us be no frail ribbon of roses!

But in contrast to this shapely elegance is the ejaculation of feeling in *Mailied* (*May Song*), where the sentences overrun the stanzas, and studied syntax gives way to the outpouring of simple exclamations:

Wie herrlich leuchtet
Mir die Natur!
Wie glänzt die Sonne!
Wie lacht die Flur!

Es dringen Blüten
Aus jedem Zweig
Und tausend Stimmen
Aus dem Gesträuch

Und Freud und Wonne
Aus jeder Brust.
O Erd', o Sonne,
O Glück, o Lust,

O Lieb', o Liebe,
So golden schön,
Wie Morgenwolken
Auf jenen Höhn,

Du segnest herrlich
Das frische Feld—
Im Blütendampfe
Die volle Welt!

O Mädchen, Mädchen,
Wie lieb' ich dich!
Wie blinkt dein Auge,
Wie liebst du mich!

How gloriously Nature shines for me! How the sun gleams! How the
meadow laughs! Blossom springs from every twig and a thousand
voices from the thickets and joy and delight from every breast. O
earth, O sun, O happiness, O bliss, O love, O love, golden and beautiful as morning clouds upon those hills, gloriously you bless the fresh
fields—in a mist of blossoms the whole world! O dear girl, dear girl,
how I love you! How your eyes sparkle, how you love me! (ll. 1–16)

Other poems imitate the style of folk-ballads, such as *Heiden-
röslein* (*Rose on the Heath*), which Herder quotes in his essay
on folk-song, and *Der König in Thule* (*The King of Thule*) which
Gretchen sings in *Faust*.

From this period also date a number of occasional poems,
letters in verse, etc, and another group of love-poems, those

concerned with Lili Schönemann, which are quite different in expressive character from the Friederike poems. Here love is not an unmitigated joy, but gives rise to a feeling of unease, of unnatural constraint: thus in the concluding line of *Neue Liebe, neues Leben* (*New Love, New Life*) Goethe cries

> Liebe, Liebe, lass mich los!

> Love, love, let me go!

2. *'Genius', creativity and individualism: the hymns*

In an important group of poems in free verse, often referred to as 'hymns', Goethe treats the theme of the genius, the heroic, exceptional individual. He is not necessarily a poet, but may be a creator (Prometheus), or a prophet (Mahomet); an anonymous 'wanderer', set apart from his fellow men; or even Ganymede, the youth who claims the gods' attention only by his exceptional beauty. What is generally stressed is his reliance on himself, on his own 'glowing' power of creativity: images of fire and warmth frequently occur.

> ... Wer half mir wider
> Der Titanen Übermut?
> Wer rettete vom Tode mich,
> Von Sklaverei?
> Hast du's nicht alles selbst vollendet,
> Heilig glühend Herz?
> Und glühtest, jung und gut,
> Betrogen, Rettungsdank
> Dem Schlafenden dadroben?

> Who helped me against the Titans' presumption? Who saved me from death, from slavery? Did you not achieve all this yourself, holy glowing heart? And did you not, young and innocent, betrayed, glow thanks for deliverance to him [Zeus] sleeping up there? (*Prometheus*, ll. 29–37)

Sometimes the genius looks upon other men with a mixture of contempt and envy, as in *Wanderers Sturmlied* (*Wanderer's Song in the Storm*), the first of the 'hymns' to be written:

> Soll der zurückkehren,
> Der kleine schwarze feurige Bauer!
> Soll der zurückkehren, erwartend
> Nur deine Gaben, Vater Bromius,
> Und helleuchtend umwärmend Feuer,
> Der kehren mutig,
> Und ich, den ihr begleitet,
> Musen und Charitinnen all,
> Den alles erwartet, was ihr,
> Musen und Charitinnen,
> Umkränzende Seligkeit
> Rings ums Leben verherrlicht habt,
> Soll mutlos kehren?

Is he to return, the small dark fiery peasant! Is he to return, awaiting only your gifts, father Bacchus, and brightly-burning all-warming fire, he to return in good spirit, and I, whom you accompany, Muses and Graces all, I whom all the engarlanding bliss awaits that you, Muses and Graces, have spread about to make life so glorious, I am to turn dispirited? (ll. 39–51)

But the creative power of the genius is also beneficial to life and to other men, as in *Mahomets-Gesang* (*Song for Mahomet*). Here the image is of a river gathering its tributaries:

> Kommt ihr alle!—
> Und nun schwillt er
> Herrlicher, ein ganz Geschlechte
> Trägt den Fürsten hoch empor,
> Und im rollenden Triumphe
> Gibt er Ländern Namen, Städte
> Werden unter seinem Fuss.

Unaufhaltsam rauscht er über,
Lässt der Türme Flammengipfel,
Marmorhäuser, eine Schöpfung
Seiner Fülle, hinter sich.

Come, all of you!—And now he swells more glorious, a whole family
bears the prince aloft, and in rolling triumph he gives countries their
names, cities spring up where he sets his foot. Unstoppable, he rushes
by, leaves the towers' flaming tops, marble houses, a creation of his
abundance, behind him. (ll. 53–63)

3. Poetic language and form

Goethe breaks the grammatical rules and 'good manners' of
eighteenth-century German to extend the expressive possibilities of the language. He creates new compounds: thus, in the
examples we have quoted, 'Blütendampf' ('blossom-vapour'),
'Rettungsdank' ('deliverance-thanks'), 'Flammengipfel' ('flame-
peaks'). He stretches conventional syntax, particularly in the
hymns: in this respect, as in their free verse form, they owe
much to Klopstock, but Goethe goes further in his innovations
than Klopstock had done. Thus, in the extract from *Prometheus* quoted above the phrase 'glühtest Rettungsdank' is a
transitive use of a normally intransitive verb, and in that from
Wanderers Sturmlied the last lines ('Den alles erwartet, was
...') are compressed and grammatically obscure. In revising
this poetry, Goethe sometimes subdued some of his more
radical innovations. Thus the original version of *Willkommen
und Abschied* (*Welcome and Farewell*) contained the lines

Die Nacht schuf tausend Ungeheuer,
Doch tausendfacher war mein Mut,

The night created a thousand monsters, but more thousandfold was
my courage,

but Goethe subsequently replaced the boldly expressive, but
grammatically impossible, comparative form 'tausendfacher'

with 'frisch und fröhlich' ('fresh and cheerful'). Similarly in *Prometheus* the newly-coined quadruple compound 'Knaben-morgenblütenträume' ('boy's-morning-blossom-dreams') was pruned of its first two elements, and some attempt was made to mitigate the dialect forms and the wildly experimental grammar of *An Schwager Kronos* (*To Coachman Time*), the original version of which is printed in *HA*. But although he toned down these early experiments, experiment with the syntactic possibilities of the German language remains a feature of Goethe's poetry at all times—particularly once more in his old age. (Cf. below, p. 98 f.).

Goethe also experiments in a variety of poetic forms and metres: song and ballad-like measures, rhymed and unrhymed, free verse and the so-called 'Knittelvers', an old-fashioned German metre with a homely, rough-hewn character (for an example, see below, p. 67.) This variety also remains a hallmark of his poetry.

C. Drama

Goethe's first major dramatic work, *Götz von Berlichingen mit der eisernen Hand* (*Götz von Berlichingen with the Iron Hand*) appeared in 1773. An earlier version, *Geschichte Gottfriedens von Berlichingen mit der eisernen Hand dramatisiert* (*The Story of Gottfried von B. . . . dramatized*) had been written in 1771, but then subjected to fairly drastic revision. Of Goethe's other major plays, both *Egmont* and *Faust* were conceived in this period, though the exact dates are unknown and both had to wait many years for completion. Of a number of minor dramatic works in various forms, the most important are *Clavigo* (1774) and *Stella* (1776), both of which are thematically of interest, and are occasionally revived on the stage today.

1. The hero and freedom

The drama was the main vehicle chosen by the 'Stürmer und

Dränger' for the presentation of their hero, the 'Kraftkerl'. Strength, vigour, forthrightness and generosity are the characteristics of Götz, the free knight,

> das Muster eines Ritters, tapfer und edel in seiner
> Freiheit, und gelassen und treu im Unglück.
>
> the model of a knight, bold and noble in his freedom, and calm and loyal in misfortune. (Elisabeth in Act IV, last scene)

Egmont is similarly introduced:

> Warum ist alle Welt dem Grafen Egmont so hold? Warum
> trügen wir ihn alle auf den Händen? Weil man ihm ansieht,
> dass er uns wohlwill; weil ihm die Fröhlichkeit, das freie
> Leben, die gute Meinung aus den Augen sieht; weil er
> nichts besitzt, das er dem Dürftigen nicht mitteilte, auch
> dem, der's nicht bedarf.
>
> Why is all the world so devoted to Count Egmont? Why would we all do anything for him? Because you can see that he means us well; because cheerfulness, a free life, a good opinion are written in his face; because he hasn't anything that he wouldn't give to a man in need, even to one that didn't need it. (Soest in Act I, first scene)

'*Freiheit*' (freedom, liberty) is the watchword of both plays. Besieged by his enemies, Götz toasts freedom with the last drops of wine in his cellar:

> GÖTZ (*Er schenkt ein*): Es geht just noch einmal herum.
> Und wenn unser Blut anfängt auf die Neige zu gehen, wie
> der Wein in dieser Flasche erst schwach, dann tropfen-
> weise rinnt, (*er tröpfelt das Letzte in sein Glas*) was soll
> unser letztes Wort sein?
> GEORG: Es lebe die Freiheit!

GÖTZ: Es lebe die Freiheit!
ALLE: Es lebe die Freiheit!

GÖTZ (*pouring out*): There is just enough to go round. And when our
blood begins to run short, as the wine in this bottle slows to a trickle,
then to a few drops (*he pours the last drops into his glass*) what shall
our last word be? GEORG: Long live liberty! GÖTZ: Long live
liberty! ALL: Long live liberty! (Act III)

Betrayed by enemies on all sides, defeated and imprisoned,
Götz does indeed die with the word on his lips:

GÖTZ: ... Arme Frau. Ich lasse dich in einer verderbten
Welt. Lerse, verlass sie nicht.—Schliesst eure Herzen
sorgfältiger als eure Tore. Es kommen die Zeiten des
Betrugs, es ist ihm Freiheit gegeben. Die Nichtswürdigen
werden regieren mit List, und der Edle wird in ihre Netze
fallen. ... Selbitz starb, und der gute Kaiser, und mein
Georg.—Gebt mir einen Trunk Wasser!—Himmlische
Luft—Freiheit! Freiheit! (*Er stirbt.*)

GÖTZ: Poor wife. I am leaving you in a corrupted world. Lerse, don't
leave her.—Close your hearts more carefully than your gates. The age
of deceit is coming, it is given its freedom. The worthless will rule by
cunning, and the noble man will be caught in their snares. ... Selbitz
is dead, and the good Emperor, and my Georg.—Give me a drink of
water! Heavenly air—Freedom! Freedom! (*Dies.*) (Act V, last scene)

Egmont too is betrayed, and led off to execution, but he
declares

... ich sterbe für die Freiheit, für die ich lebte und focht,
und der ich mich jetzt leidend opfre.

I die for liberty, for which I lived and fought, and to which I now in
suffering sacrifice myself. (Act V, last scene)

But though Egmont's death is symbolically the *beginning* of the Netherlands' struggle against Spanish oppression, which ultimately results in a new liberty, it also marks like Götz's death the *end* of a period of traditional liberties of the old style. In both *Götz* and *Egmont* Goethe seems more concerned with personal freedom—the freedom for the heroic individual to live his own life—than with liberty in a political sense: the German word 'Freiheit' makes no distinction. The ambiguity, and the dubious morality, of Goethe's concept of freedom has been the basis of recurrent adverse criticism. Some critics—chiefly Marxists—have stressed the political libertarian element in *Egmont* and the importance in that play of the sympathy between the hero and the people; but Goethe's portrait of the people is hardly flattering to their political intelligence or resolution.

Though he is not a man of action like Götz or Egmont, Faust too is conceived as a heroic individual who longs for freedom, who regards the study which forms his world as a prison confining his adventurous spirit. Thus in his opening monologue, one of the scenes already present in the so-called *Urfaust* manuscript of *circa* 1775 (cf. below, p. 76), he cries:

> Weh! steck ich in dem Kerker noch?
> Verfluchtes dumpfes Mauerloch,
> Wo selbst das liebe Himmelslicht
> Trüb durch gemalte Scheiben bricht!

Alas! am I still in this prison? Accursed, gloomy walled-up hole, where even the blessed light of heaven is dully scattered by the painted panes! (*Urfaust*, ll. 45–8; cf. *Faust I*, ll. 398–401)

Like Götz and Egmont, Faust draws strength from Nature; and in a line which appears in the *Urfaust* manuscript but is already deleted in the first published version of the work, the *Fragment* of 1790, Faust proclaims to his pedantic 'famulus' Wagner the 'Sturm und Drang' slogan

Mein Herr Magister, hab' Er Kraft!

My learned friend, what you need is vigour! (*Urfaust*, l. 195)

2. Love

The theme of love, in particular that of the lover's constancy or inconstancy, which clearly carries a considerable weight of personal emotion for Goethe, plays an important subsidiary role in *Götz*, *Egmont* and *Faust*. In *Götz* Weislingen betrays Marie for Adelheid, who in turn betrays him for Franz. In *Egmont* Klärchen is placed between her devotion to the heroic Egmont and the devotion to her of the unheroic Brackenburg. Into *Faust* Goethe introduces the episode of Faust's love for Gretchen, which forms no part of any previous treatment of the Faust legend: the 'Gretchen tragedy' is the only part of *Faust* to have attained any definite shape at this period (cf. below, p. 76 and p. 80). In *Clavigo* and *Stella*, within the smaller confines of the domestic drama, the theme of love can come to the fore: in its original, non-tragic version *Stella* is subtitled *Ein Schauspiel für Liebende* (*A Play for Lovers*). *Claudine von Villa Bella*, a 'Singspiel' (play in prose with musical numbers) completed in 1775, shows two brothers in rivalry for the same girl—a favourite plot of the 'Stürmer und Dränger'.

3. Tragedy

Götz is not subtitled 'tragedy', but simply 'Schauspiel' ('play'), probably in token of its revolt against the eighteenth-century 'rules' of the drama, of which the separation of the genres was one. But it ends on a note of gloom:

> GÖTZ: . . . Freiheit! Freiheit! (*Er stirbt.*)
> ELISABETH: Nur droben, droben bei dir. Die Welt ist ein Gefängnis.
> MARIA: Edler Mann! Edler Mann! Wehe dem Jahrhundert, das dich von sich stiess!
> LERSE: Wehe der Nachkommenschaft, die dich verkennt!

GÖTZ: ... Freedom! Freedom! (*Dies.*) ELIZABETH: Only in Heaven, in Heaven where you are. The world is a prison. MARIA: Noble man! Noble man! Woe to the century that spurned you! LERSE: Woe to the posterity that does not recognize you!

Yet *Götz* is possibly Goethe's only wholly tragic work. *Egmont* and *Clavigo* are both subtitled 'Trauerspiel' (tragedy), but in *Egmont* the prison seems at the end to disappear, and the hero, who is in fact being led off to execution, strides out boldly towards the Spanish soldiers as if in battle. At times—in the scene with the Secretary in Act II, and in his conversation with Ferdinand in Act V—Egmont seems to speak as a man aware of an inexorable tragic destiny, and in Book 20 of *Dichtung und Wahrheit*, written in 1813, Goethe speaks of *Egmont* as an attempt to give dramatic shape to his conception of this force of destiny, which he terms 'das Dämonische' ('the daemonic'). Yet he describes this mysterious power as 'wohlwollend' ('benevolent'), by no means necessarily tragic. (Cf. the poem *Urworte. Orphisch*, written in 1817: see p. 92 below.) In the conclusion of *Clavigo* too, Ronald Peacock (in his book *Goethe's Major Plays*) detects a hint of 'Verklärung' ('transfiguration') characteristic of Goethe's peculiar conciliatory endings rather than of tragedy proper. One might argue that many tragedies do in fact end on a note of hope that the bloodletting will bring about a better state of affairs. But it is undoubtedly the case that Goethe's later plays end on an optimistic, conciliatory or ambiguous note. Erich Heller has written in *The Disinherited Mind* of 'Goethe and the Avoidance of Tragedy' (with particular reference to *Iphigenie* and *Faust*). *Stella* provides a most remarkable instance. Very little alteration was needed for Goethe in 1806 to turn *Stella* into an orthodox 'domestic tragedy' like Lessing's *Miss Sara Sampson*: the hero, Fernando, torn in his love between Cäcilie and Stella, shoots himself and Stella dies. But in the original version the three are reconciled and, are, it appears, ready to live on in a *ménage a trois*. Quite apart from the morality of *Stella*, the

B

ambiguous or ambivalent endings of Goethe's plays have always been a subject of critical debate and dissension, as indeed has their unorthodox form in general.

4. *Dramatic form*

German drama in the eighteenth century had still largely been bound by the 'rules' of the seventeenth-century French theatre, albeit less rigorously applied than in the heyday of French classicism. Goethe's major plays are all experimental in form—*Clavigo* and *Stella*, their endings apart, being the most conventional.

In *Götz* Goethe is imitating what he and Herder imagined to be the *Shakespearian* manner. He defies with gusto both the rule of the 'Three Unities', and that of 'propriety' or 'decorum' (in classical French terminology, *bienséance*) which forbade violent action and violent language on the stage. It may be observed that Goethe knew nothing of the conditions of performance of Shakespeare's plays, the English type of open stage being unknown in Germany: Goethe assumed that Shakespeare wrote with as little regard for the practical exigencies of the stage as he himself did. *Egmont* is much more restrained than *Götz* and here long years of gestation made their mark, but it is still profoundly unclassical. There is no real plot: we merely see the hero presented, directly and indirectly, in different situations and from different points of view. And in the Gretchen tragedy in *Faust* Goethe is using another unorthodox dramatic technique: that which Herder had taught him to see in the *ballad*. The story is not told in its entirety, but moves by what Herder called 'Sprünge und Würfe' ('leaps and bounds'), leaving the audience to fill in the details. This was an important innovation. Goethe's contemporary, Lenz, also used this technique, and Georg Büchner took it up in his *Woyzeck* (1837); but it was not until the twentieth century that it became popular. In contrast to the 'closed' form of the classical theatre,

'Shakespearian' and ballad form are 'open', and both are ancestors of Brecht's 'non-Aristotelian', 'epic' drama.

The term *'lyric'* is sometimes applied to Goethe's dramatic work in contrasting its techniques with those of more conventional drama. R. Peacock argues that this is 'too general a term' for works which 'grow out of a vivid sense of reality, not of lyric dream or feeling. It is essential to accept them as showing by nature the proper stuff of drama, and then to analyse their special unorthodoxy.' (*Goethe's Major Plays*, pp. 2–3.) The reader must however be closely attentive to such poetic detail as the repetition of symbol, image or word-pattern which Goethe uses to unify his plays: the symbol of the horse in *Egmont*, for example, or the dense verbal texture of a later play like *Tasso*. Poetic drama, of course, always uses associative patterns of this kind; but Goethe does perhaps rely more heavily on these than on techniques of external action, of climax and tension in the traditional dramatic sense.

Most of the completed plays of these years are in prose, but a number of different verse-forms are employed, and the *Urfaust* sketches include both prose and verse scenes.

D. The novel

Goethe's first novel, *Die Leiden des jungen Werther* (traditionally translated *The Sorrows of Young Werther*, but 'Leiden' means more nearly 'sufferings'), appeared in 1775. It immediately achieved tremendous fame: for much of his life Goethe remained to most of his contemporaries 'the author of Werther'. Much of the work's notoriety is attributable to its transparent, and many felt shameless, use of factual material: real-life episodes involving Goethe himself and some of his friends, and the suicide of K. W. Jerusalem, son of a prominent German theologian of the time. This is of subordinate importance, but the novel does contain a powerfully-felt personal content and is one of Goethe's most emotional works.

1. Emotion

Werther is often called sentimental, but it is also a study of sentimentality—that is, of an indulgence in emotion, an excess of emotion allowed to dominate the entire personality. Goethe prefaced the second edition with verses to this effect, concluding 'Sei ein Mann und folge mir nicht nach'—'Be a man and do not follow my example.'

> Bester Freund, was ist das Herz des Menschen!
>
> Dearest friend, what is the heart of man!

This is the second sentence of the novel, and the dominating word 'Herz' recurs again and again throughout the work. A year after the beginning of the action, in the course of his unsuccessful attempt to break away from his fatal love, Werther still writes of

> dies Herz, das doch mein einziger Stolz ist, das ganz allein die Quelle von allem ist, aller Kraft, aller Seligkeit und alles Elendes.
>
> this heart, that after all is still my only pride, that is the one and only source of everything, of all my strength, of all my joy and of all my wretchedness. (Book II, letter of 9 May)

And a month later:

> . . . ich will nur Lotten wieder näher, das ist alles. Und ich lache über mein eignes Herz—und tu' ihm seinen Willen.
>
> . . . I only want to be nearer Lotte again, that's all. And I laugh at my own heart—and let it have its way. (Book II, letter of 18 June)

Werther is unbalanced because he lives entirely by his heart: as his love, impossible of fulfilment, consumes his heart, so it consumes all his energies. It is a fatal disease.

Du gibst mir zu, wir nennen das eine Krankheit zum Tode,
wodurch die Natur so angegriffen wird, dass teils ihre
Kräfte verzehrt, teils so ausser Wirkung gesetzt werden,
dass sie sich nicht wieder aufzuhelfen, durch keine
glückliche Revolution den gewöhnlichen Umlauf des
Lebens wieder herzustellen fähig ist. Nun, mein Lieber,
lass uns das auf den Geist anwenden. Sieh den Menschen
an in seiner Eingeschränktheit, wie Eindrücke auf ihn
wirken, Ideen sich bei ihn festsetzen, bis endlich eine
wachsende Leidenschaft ihn aller ruhigen Sinneskraft
beraubt und ihn zugrunde richtet.

You will admit, we speak of a sickness unto death when we mean
something that attacks our nature in such a way that its energies are
partly wasted, partly made so ineffectual, that it cannot be helped any
more, cannot restore by any fortunate revolution the normal course
of life. Now, my friend, let us apply this to the spirit. Look at man,
limited as he is, see how impressions influence him, ideas become
fixed in his mind, until finally a growing passion robs him of all power
of sane reflexion and destroys him. (Book I, letter of 12 August)

We note the words *Kraft*, *Kräfte* again. Werther is a kind of
'Kraftmensch' too, and he too longs for freedom from
'Einschränkung' ('limitation'). But his energies can find only
one outlet, and when that is barred to him they are turned
self-destructively inwards.

Werther enthuses over nature (but see above, p. 15) and
over the simple, unaffected, idyllic life of country people. He is
irked by artificiality and formality, and fares ill in aristocratic
society. The novel portrays a world in which a sincere and
sensitive individual can find no place. A Marxist critic such
as Lukács naturally seeks an interpretation whereby the
'Einschränkung' from which Werther suffers is primarily a
social frustration, caused objectively by the conditions of
feudal-aristocratic society. But Werther's attitude to nature and
society is essentially a sentimental one—irrespective of whether
his view of the aristocracy, for example, is objectively correct or

not. That is, his attitude is formed out of books and serves
above all to feed his current emotional state. His reaction to his
brush with aristocratic society in Book II illustrates this.

> Ich strich mich sacht aus der vornehmen Gesellschaft, ging,
> setzte mich in ein Kabriolett und fuhr nach M . . , dort
> vom Hügel die Sonne untergehen zu sehen und dabei in
> meinem Homer den herrlichen Gesang zu lesen, wie Ulyss
> von dem trefflichen Schweinehirten bewirtet wird.

I crept quietly out of their fine society, went and sat myself in a
cabriolet and drove to M . . ., to watch from the hill there while the
sun went down and to read in my Homer the glorious passage in
which Odysseus is cared for by the noble swineherd. (Book II, letter
of 15 March)

2. Form

Werther is the first really significant German contribution to
the modern novel. The epistolary form was well known in the
eighteenth century, but Goethe gives us only Werther's own
letters, not the replies to them. This emphasizes his isolation,
giving the work the character of a monologue in which one is,
however, made aware of interruptions by the reactions they
produce:

> Ich bitte dich, lieber Wilhelm, es war gewiss nicht auf dich
> geredet, wenn ich die Menschen unerträglich schalt, die
> von uns Ergebung in unvermeidliche Schicksale fordern . . .

Please, my dear Wilhelm, I certainly did not mean you when I said
that I could not bear the sort of people who are always insisting that
we submit to the inevitable . . . . (Book I, letter of 8 August)

> Und daran seid ihr alle schuld, die ihr mich in das Joch
> geschwatzt und mir so viel von Aktivität vorgesungen habt.

And it's your fault, all of you who talked me into this drudgery, and
went on preaching to me about finding something to occupy me.
(Book II, letter of 24 December 1771)

The novel is concentrated, short by eighteenth-century standards, and its precise time-scale should be noted, together with the way in which the changing seasons reflect the hero's moods. Characteristic of the 'sentimental' age is the use of literary reference to establish emotional moods: Goldsmith's *Vicar of Wakefield*, Klopstock's ode on the thunderstorm, Lessing's *Emilia Galotti* which Werther (like Jerusalem in fact) leaves open on his desk when he shoots himself,[1] and above all Homer and Ossian. As Goethe observed to Henry Crabb Robinson in 1829, 'Werther praised Homer while he retained his senses, and Ossian when he was going mad.' The remark is, of course, ironical; but Homer does stand for life and health while Ossian represents and fosters a mood of melancholy, gloom and despair.

[1] In England, the *Gentleman's Magazine* related in November 1784 the sad case of a young lady who had carried the chain-reaction one stage further: she was found dead in bed with a copy of *Werther* under the pillow.

3

The early years in Weimar:
1775–1786

A. General characterization

1. A time of transition

The years Goethe spent in Weimar before his journey to Italy
were a period of transition in his creative life. He moved into a
social atmosphere of refinement and culture, and his work
reflects this both in its content and in its increasingly restrained,
more 'classical' form. But at the same time there was still
quite a lot of the 'Stürmer und Dränger' in him, which found
its main outlet in a variety of escapades with the young Duke:
drinking, hunting, skating and playing practical jokes. In 1782
Goethe wrote a poem on the death of Johann Martin Mieding,
carpenter and stage-manager of the amateur theatrical perform-
ances which took place at court. In this he alludes to the dual
character of this period of his life:

> O Weimar! dir fiel ein besonder Los:
> Wie Bethlehem in Juda, klein und gross!
> Bald wegen Geist und Witz beruft dich weit
> Europens Mund, bald wegen Albernheit.
> Der stille Weise schaut und sieht geschwind,
> Wie zwei Extreme nah verschwistert sind.

O Weimar! yours was an unusual destiny: like Bethlehem in Judaea,
little and great! Now on account of wit and good taste you are famed
throughout Europe, now on account of childish pranks. Quietly the
wise man looks on and soon sees how two extremes can be closely
related. (*Auf Miedings Tod*, ll. 39–44)

Goethe's attachment to Charlotte von Stein during these years exerted a considerable restraining influence upon him. Barker Fairley, in *A Study of Goethe*, stresses the importance of this relationship in rescuing Goethe from the destructive, Wertherian excesses to which his emotional nature naturally tended. In the works of this period the earlier individualism gives way to an ethical humanism and a growing sense of responsibility to others, to society, and to life as a whole.

Goethe's public duties, which included a measure of responsibility for the Duchy's roads and mines, led him to take a new kind of interest in his surroundings: this phase of his life marks the beginning of his *scientific* activities. The place of 'mere' poetry amongst the varied constituents of 'real' life becomes problematic. This is one aspect of the theme of *Torquato Tasso*; and although the period produced some important lyric poetry, Goethe did in fact complete no important large-scale work between his arrival in Weimar and his departure for Italy, unless we are to count the prose version of *Iphigenie auf Tauris* (1779). *Iphigenie* was versified in Italy, and *Torquato Tasso*, begun in 1780, was not finished until after his return, in 1789. Though one may call these works in their final form products of Goethe's classical period, I shall discuss them in the present chapter, since I regard them as belonging in spirit essentially to the phase in which they were conceived. Their 'classical' formal perfection represents only the achievement of a style which Goethe was already moving towards before the Italian journey.

2. '*Mässigung*'

The value of 'Mässigung' ('moderation') is frequently stressed at this period. Thus in one of the most famous of the poems addressed to Charlotte, Goethe asserts that she

> Tropftest Mässigung dem heissen Blute,

> infused my fevered blood with moderation ('Warum gabst du uns die tiefen Blicke...': cf. below, p. 41)

In *Iphigenie* the heroine names lack of 'Mässigung' as one of the characteristics which led the descendants of Tantalus repeatedly into tragedy:

> ... doch es schmiedete
> Der Gott um ihre Stirn ein ehern Band.
> Rat, Mässigung und Weisheit und Geduld
> Verbarg er ihrem scheuen, düstern Blick:
> Zur Wut ward ihnen jegliche Begier,
> Und grenzenlos drang ihre Wut umher.

> But the god forged a brazen band about their forehead. Good counsel, moderation, wisdom and patience he hid from their dark, furtive glance: their every desire became a frenzy, and their frenzy drove them about beyond all boundaries. (Act I, sc. 3)

And in *Tasso*, Antonio, who identifies himself as 'der Mässige' ('the moderate man', Act II, scene 3), sees the lack of this quality as the source of Tasso's delusions:

> Es ist gewiss, ein ungemässigt Leben,
> Wie es uns schwere wilde Träume gibt,
> Macht uns zuletzt am hellen Tage träumen.

> For sure, an immoderate way of life, as it gives us wild and fearful dreams, ends up by making us dream in broad daylight. (Act V, sc. 1)

We even find a poem accepting the 'Einschränkung' or limitation which Werther found so intolerable. Here again 'das rechte Mass' is the key.

> Ich weiss nicht, was mir hier gefällt,
> In dieser engen kleinen Welt
> Mit holdem Zauberband mich hält.
> Vergess' ich doch, vergess' ich gern,
> Wie seltsam mich das Schicksal leitet;

Und ach, ich fühle, nah und fern
Ist mir noch manches zubereitet.
O wäre doch das rechte Mass getroffen!
Was bleibt mir nun, als eingehüllt,
Von holder Lebenskraft erfüllt,
In stiller Gegenwart die Zukunft zu erhoffen!

I do not know what pleases me here, in this narrow little world keeps me in tender magic bonds. I don't remember, I don't want to remember how strangely fate guides me; and oh, I feel, near and far, much is still awaiting me. O if only the right measure were struck! What can I do now but, cocooned, filled with tender life-giving energy, in the quiet present await the future! (*Einschränkung*)

B. Lyric poetry

The poetry of the years 1775-86 continues to treat the themes of man and his powers (as in the 'hymns'), of nature and of love. But in all these spheres we find the 'Mässigung', the moderation of attitude characteristic of this epoch.

1. Man and the divine

The earlier series of 'hymns' may be said to conclude with *Seefahrt* (*Sea Voyage*) and *Harzreise im Winter* (*Journey through the Harz in Winter*). These are far less defiant in their self-reliance than *Prometheus*, far less egoistic than *Ganymed*, far less impatient than *An Schwager Kronos*. *Harzreise* in particular suggests a sympathetic concern with the affairs of other men, rather than the previous isolation of the 'genius'. Then comes another group of 'hymns', also concerned with man and his place in the universe, but stressing not so much his powers as his *limitations*. One of them indeed bears the title *Grenzen der Menschheit* (*Limitations of Man*):

Denn mit Göttern
Soll sich nicht messen
Irgend ein Mensch.

Hebt er sich aufwärts
Und berührt
Mit dem Scheitel die Sterne,
Nirgends haften dann
Die unsichren Sohlen,
Und mit ihm spielen
Wolken und Winde.

For no human being ought to measure himself against gods. If he
lifts himself up and makes his head touch the stars, then nowhere has
he firm footing, and clouds and winds play with him. (ll. 11–20)

The *Gesang der Geister über den Wassern* (*Song of the Spirits
above the Waters*) repeats this theme. And in the play *Iphigenie*
the heroine recalls a 'Song of the Fates' which (in the same
verse form as the 'Weimar hymns') holds up the fate of Tantalus
as a grim warning to any man presumptuous enough to 'measure himself against gods':

Es fürchte die Götter
Das Menschengeschlecht!
Sie halten die Herrschaft
In ewigen Händen,
Und können sie brauchen,
Wie's ihnen gefällt . . .

Let mankind fear the gods! They hold power in eternal hands, and
can use it as they please. (*Iphigenie auf Tauris*, end of Act IV)

Yet 'measured against' earthly standards, man has tremendous
power—and the responsibility to his fellow-men that goes with
it. Man's distinction is his autonomy as a moral being. And so
the poem *Das Göttliche* (*The Divine*) is not about the gods at all
but about man:

Edel sei der Mensch,
Hilfreich und gut!

Denn das allein
Unterscheidet ihn
Von allen Wesen,
Die wir kennen.

Let man be noble, helpful and good! For that alone distinguishes him
from all the creatures that we know. (ll. 1–6)

2. Nature

The naïve joy in nature expressed in a poem like *Mailied* is
here replaced by other attitudes. Characteristic is a yearning
for peace and tranquillity, as in the two short poems (one
written in 1776, the other in 1780) which bear the title *Wanderers
Nachtlied* (*Wanderer's Song at Night*).

(i)

Der du von dem Himmel bist,
Alles Leid und Schmerzen stillest,
Den, der doppelt elend ist,
Doppelt mit Erquickung füllest,
—Ach, ich bin des Treibens müde,
Was soll all der Schmerz und Lust?—
Süsser Friede,
Komm, ach komm in meine Brust!

You who come from heaven, who still all sorrow and pain, who fill
him who is doubly wretched with a doubly refreshing draught—ah, I
am tired of this restlessness, why all this pain and joy?—sweet peace,
come, ah, come into my breast.

(ii)

Über allen Gipfeln
Ist Ruh,
In allen Wipfeln
Spürest du
Kaum einen Hauch;
Die Vögelein schweigen im Walde.

Warte nur, balde
Ruhest du auch.

Over all the mountain-tops is peace, in all the treetops you detect
scarcely a breath; the little birds are silent in the woods. Only wait,
soon you will also be at peace.

But nature also presents hostile aspects: this too is new. In
Willkommen und Abschied (1771) the lover braves terrors of
the night which are in any case only imaginary:

Die Nacht schuf tausend Ungeheuer,
Doch frisch und fröhlich war mein Mut.

The night created a thousand monsters, but my spirit was fresh
and gay.

And in the gypsies' song in the original version of *Götz*, the
werewolves run away when called by their real names. In the
ballad *Erlkönig* of 1782, the father similarly tells his frightened
child that the Elf-king (or Alder-king) is not real.

Wer reitet so spät durch Nacht und Wind?
Es ist der Vater mit seinem Kind;
Er hat den Knaben wohl in dem Arm,
Er fasst ihn sicher, er hält ihn warm.—

Mein Sohn, was birgst du so bang dein Gesicht?—
Siehst, Vater, du den Erlkönig nicht?
Den Erlenkönig mit Kron' und Schweif?—
Mein Sohn, es ist ein Nebelstreif.—

Who is it riding so late through the night and the wind? It is the
father with his child. He has the boy safe in his arms, he holds him
tight and keeps him warm.—My son, why are you frightened and
hiding your face?—Father, don't you see the Elf-king? The Elf-king
with his crown and his train?—My son, it's just a wisp of fog. (ll. 1–8)

But at the end of the poem the Elf-king proves his power:

„Ich liebe dich, mich reizt deine schöne Gestalt;
Und bist du nicht willig, so brauch' ich Gewalt."—
Mein Vater, mein Vater, jetzt fasst er mich an!
Erlkönig hat mir ein Leids getan!—

Dem Vater grauset's, er reitet geschwind,
Er hält in Armen das ächzende Kind,
Erreicht den Hof mit Mühe und Not;
In seinen Armen das Kind war tot.

'I love you, your beautiful shape charms me; and if you won't come,
I shall use force.'—Father, father, now he's taking hold of me! Elf-
king has hurt me!—The father shudders, he hurries along, he holds
in his arms the groaning child, just manages to reach the farm; in his
arms the child was dead. (ll. 25–32)

3. Love

The poems to and for Charlotte von Stein ('Lida') reflect the
soothing influence of their relationship. Its essence is expressed
in the untitled poem beginning 'Warum gabst du uns die tiefen
Blicke' ('Why did you give us these deep insights . . .'), written
in 1776 as a letter to Charlotte and never published by Goethe:

Ach, so viele tausend Menschen kennen,
Dumpf sich treibend, kaum ihr eigen Herz,
Schweben zwecklos hin und her und rennen
Hoffnungslos in unversehnem Schmerz;
Jauchzen wieder, wenn der schnellen Freuden
Unerwart'te Morgenröte tagt.
Nur uns armen liebevollen beiden
Ist das wechselseit'ge Glück versagt,
Uns zu lieben, ohn' uns zu verstehen,
In dem andern sehn, was er nie war,
Immer frisch auf Traumglück auszugehen
Und zu schwanken auch in Traumgefahr.

Ah, so many thousand human beings, driven on by obscure instinct,
scarcely know their own heart, hover aimlessly this way and that and
run about hopeless in unforeseen pain; rejoice again, when there

dawns the unexpected day of rapid joys. Only to us two, poor loving pair, is the mutual happiness denied of loving without understanding, of seeing in the other what he never was, of setting out ever fresh in search of a dream of happiness and of wavering even in a dream of danger. (ll. 9–20)

The poem stresses the differentness of this love, stresses how unlike the common experience of love it is. Nocturnal imagery also appears in this poetry, as in the two 'Wanderer' poems quoted above (p. 39 f.). The image of the tranquil moon is used in the well-known *An den Mond* (*To the Moon*) and in *Jägers Abendlied* (*Huntsman's Serenade*), and is associated with the character of the Princess in *Tasso* (by Leonore in Act III).

4. 'Sehnsucht'

One group of poems written during these years presents a rather different character. These are the songs put into the mouth of Mignon in *Wilhelm Meister*, which express not a desire for peace and contentment as such, but a passionate yearning ('Sehnsucht'). In Mignon the yearning is associated with Italy, her native land; and it was only when he too went to Italy and found there a different concept of 'das rechte Mass' that Goethe's dissatisfaction was for the moment genuinely stilled:

> Kennst du das Land, wo die Zitronen blühn,
> Im dunkeln Laub die Goldorangen glühn,
> Ein sanfter Wind vom blauen Himmel weht,
> Die Myrte still und hoch der Lorbeer steht,
> Kennst du es wohl?
> > Dahin! Dahin
> Möcht' ich mit dir, o mein Geliebter, ziehn!

Do you know the land where the lemon-trees blossom, where in the dark foliage the golden oranges glow, where a gentle breeze blows from the blue sky, where the calm myrtle and the tall laurel stand, do you know it, I wonder? There, there I should like to go with you, my lover. (*Mignon*, i, ll. 1–6; originally in *Wilhelm Meisters theatralische Sendung*, Book IV, ch. i)

C. Drama

Iphigenie auf Tauris and *Torquato Tasso*, the two major dramatic works conceived during the early Weimar years, treat different but related problems. *Iphigenie* is concerned with morality in general and with the relationship of man and the gods, *Tasso* with the position of the artist in society. Both are, in their different ways, about the relation of the individual to the outside world, and a number of common themes and motifs can be observed. Their common biographical background is evident in that the figure of Charlotte von Stein has influenced Goethe's portrayal both of Iphigenie and of the Princess in *Tasso*, and the whole situation and setting of the latter play is, of course, reminiscent of that of Goethe's life at Weimar. The two plays are also very similar in form.

1. Iphigenie: the moral world

In 1802 Goethe sent Schiller a copy of *Iphigenie*, wryly observing that the play was 'verteufelt human' ('confoundedly humane') and Schiller thought it 'erstaunlich modern und ungriechisch' ('astoundingly modern and un-Greek'). Comparison of Goethe's play with Euripides' *Iphigenia in Tauris* shows that for Goethe the gods, the curse, the oracle, the Furies who pursue Orest, have lost their objective validity, and what matters is human interpretations of and attitudes towards them; while Thoas, who for the Greeks was simply a barbarian, is 'ein edler Mann' ('a noble man'). It is human nobility and Iphigenie's truthfulness that triumph, not (as in Euripides' play), cunning, trickery, force of arms or, when all else fails, direct intervention of the gods.

> Gewalt und List, der Männer höchster Ruhm,
> Wird durch die Wahrheit dieser hohen Seele
> Beschämt, und reines kindliches Vertrauen
> Zu einem edlen Manne wird belohnt.

Force and cunning, the highest glory of men, is shamed by the truthfulness of this lofty soul, and pure childlike trust in a noble man is
rewarded. (Orest in Act V, sc. 6)

The gods do not extricate man from his difficulties by direct
miraculous intervention in his affairs:

Sie pflegen Menschen menschlich zu erretten.

They are accustomed to save human beings by human agency (Arkas
in Act IV, sc. 2)

Man must demonstrate the existence of divine qualities himself, as enjoined by the poem *Das Göttliche*. But this means that
the interpretation of the divine will is a matter of human subjectivity, and it may often happen that, as Orest tells Pylades,

Mit seltner Kunst flichtst du der Götter Rat
Und deine Wünsche klug in eins zusammen.

With rare art you weave the counsels of the gods and your own
wishes cleverly together (II, 1)

What criterion has man to judge by?

THOAS: Es spricht kein Gott, es spricht dein eignes Herz.
IPHIGENIE: Sie reden nur durch unser Herz zu uns.

THOAS: It is not a god speaking, it is your own heart. IPHIGENIE: They
speak to us only through our heart. (I, 3)

Iphigenie is associated with truth and purity of soul: again
and again we find expressions such as 'Wahrheit', 'hohe Seele',
'rein', used in connexion with her, as in our first quotation.
Amongst the other characters, Pylades above all represents
the practical wisdom of the world ('Klugheit'). Iphigenie's
values are absolutes: in real life it may prove impossible or

even dangerous to insist on them. Such is at all events the view of Pylades:

> So wirst du, reine Seele, dich und uns
> Zugrunde richten.

In this way you, pure soul, will be your own ruin and ours. (IV, 4)

Iphigenie however insists that

> Ganz unbefleckt geniesst sich nur das Herz.

Literally, 'The heart can only enjoy (or "savour") itself when quite without spot'. The effect of self-righteousness, of moral self-indulgence, is less strong in the original version of this line, 'Ganz unbefleckt ist nur die Seele ruhig' ('The soul is only calm when quite without spot'). To this Pylades replies

> So hast du dich im Tempel wohl bewahrt;
> Das Leben lehrt uns, weniger mit uns
> Und andern strenge sein: du lernst es auch.
> So wunderbar ist dies Geschlecht gebildet,
> So vielfach ist's verschlungen und verknüpft,
> Dass keiner in sich selbst, noch mit den andern
> Sich rein und unverworren halten kann.
> Auch sind wir nicht bestellt, uns selbst zu richten . . .

So you may have kept yourself in the temple; life teaches us to be less severe on ourselves and on others: you will learn that too. So wondrously is this race formed, joined and intertwined in so many ways, that no man can keep himself pure and unconfused, either in himself or with others. Nor are we called upon to be our own judges . . . (IV, 4)

It is debatable how much weight Goethe intends us to give to Pylades' arguments. The outcome of the play does seem to justify Iphigenie's conduct and the enormous risk she takes. Erich Heller contends that this outcome is

not dramatically true, which is as much as to say that it
has the truth of a vision of what life and the world could
be if they corresponded to what is best in a great and good
soul. It is dramatically not true because the objective
world which is the scene of the play is not real enough to
offer serious resistance to the realization of that vision.
(*Goethe and the Avoidance of Tragedy*)

Most critics, favourable or unfavourable, seem to agree that the
moral vision of the play is to be identified with the standpoint
of the heroine. But Roy Pascal has stressed the role of Pylades
as representative of the 'objective world' beyond the temple
precincts, in his essay in *The Era of Goethe* (see Bibliography).

In the traditional Greek story, Orest is pursued by the Furies.
But Goethe's Orest, as Pylades tells him,

nimmst das Amt der Furien auf dich.

You take the Furies' office upon yourself. (II, 1)

Orest is morbid, paralysed by his own *feeling* of guilt, a sick
man—he refers to himself as 'verpestet' ('plague-stricken'); the
mysterious process of Act III is commonly called 'die Heilung
des Orest'—'The healing of Orest', and Pylades indeed greets
Iphigenie in Act IV with the words 'Dein Bruder ist geheilt'
('your brother is healed', or 'cured'). The motif of 'Heilschlaf'
or healing sleep occurs elsewhere in Goethe's works—notably
in *Egmont* (Act V, prison scene), and in the opening scene of
Faust II, completed in 1827, where natural forces exercise a
healing influence on the man who has been subject to great
emotional strain, irrespective of his guilt or innocence:

Wenn der Blüten Frühlingsregen
Über alle schwebend sinkt,
Wenn der Felder grüner Segen

Allen Erdgebornen blinkt,
Kleiner Elfen Geistergrösse
Eilet, wo sie helfen kann,
Ob er heilig, ob er böse,
Jammert sie der Unglücksmann.

When the spring rain of blossoms floats down over all, when the
green blessing of the fields shines on all earth-born creatures, small
elves' great spiritual power hurries to where it can be of aid; whether
he be a saint or a sinner, they are sorry for the unlucky man. (*Faust* ll.
4613 ff.)

2. *Tasso: the artist in society*

Goethe is said to have defined the theme of *Tasso* as 'die
Disproportion des Talents mit dem Leben' ('the incompatibility
of talent and life'). Tasso is at odds with the world around him;
like Orest he is spoken of as a sick man, whom the other
characters are anxious to cure:

> Besser wär's,
> Wenn wir ihn heilen könnten, lieber gleich
> Auf treuen Rat des Arztes eine Kur
> Versuchten, dann mit dem Geheilten froh
> Den neuen Weg des frischen Lebens gingen.

It would be better if we could heal him, rather straight away followed
the doctor's faithful advice and attempted a cure, then when he was
healed cheerfully set out on the new way of fresh life. (Alfons in Act I,
sc. 2)

The images of the doctor, of medicine and of healing recur
throughout the play, but whether or not Tasso is ultimately
cured—or curable—is open to dispute. Many critics see Tasso's
fate as specifically bound up with his nature as a creative
artist—thus E. M. Wilkinson in her study 'Goethe's *Torquato
Tasso*. The Tragedy of the Poet' (1946, now reprinted in *Goethe,
Poet and Thinker*), and W. Rasch, *Goethes 'Torquato Tasso'.
Die Tragödie des Dichters* (1954). On the other hand, Goethe
himself retrospectively linked Tasso with Werther; and although

Werther has artistic ambitions, this fact is not generally held to
be of such vital significance. Josef Kunz, in his commentary on
Tasso in the *HA*, also links Tasso with Orest, as a character
who makes absolute demands on reality—whereas Antonio, like
Pylades and a number of other Goethean characters down to
the Captain in *Die Wahlverwandtschaften*, is prepared to live
life on its own terms. The artist is thus perhaps only to be
taken as a particular instance of a general human type. Antonio
characterizes Tasso thus:

> Er fordert das Unmögliche von sich,
> Damit er es von andern fordern dürfe.
> Die letzten Enden aller Dinge will
> Sein Geist zusammenfassen; das gelingt
> Kaum einem unter Millionen Menschen,
> Und er ist nicht der Mann: er fällt zuletzt,
> Um nichts gebessert, in sich selbst zurück.

> He asks the impossible of himself, so that he can claim the right to
> ask it of others. His spirit seeks to comprehend the ultimate limits
> of all things; scarcely one man in millions can succeed in that, and
> he is not the man; at last, having gained nothing by it, he falls back
> into himself. (III, 4)

The question which has been raised in connexion with the
figure of Pylades in *Iphigenie* must also be asked of *Tasso*. Are
we to see and judge the action entirely from the point of view of
the titular protagonist, or are we to take seriously the attitude
to the play's central problem embodied in the other characters?
Tasso presents us with an established society, governed by a
code of conduct. All the characters except Tasso accept the
values of this society. To it Tasso opposes the ideal of a Golden
Age, in which

> Erlaubt ist, was gefällt.

> Whatever is pleasing is permitted. (II, 1)

The Princess replies that in actual society

> Erlaubt ist, was sich ziemt.

> Whatever is fitting is permitted.

This antithesis is developed in detail. The formulae are echoed in the quarrel between Tasso and Antonio:

> ANTONIO: Es ziemt der hohe Ton, die rasche Glut
> Nicht dir zu mir, noch dir an diesem Orte.
> TASSO: Was du dir hier erlaubst, das ziemt auch mir.

> ANTONIO: This haughty tone, this hot, quick temper does not come fittingly from you to me, nor from you in this place. TASSO: What you permit yourself here is fitting for me too. (II, 3)

Any interpretation of the difficult and ambivalent final scene must rest on the degree of validity the critic is prepared to grant to the demands of society as opposed to those of the hero. Those who see Tasso as a tragic figure are inclined to see the society which surrounds Tasso, and the demands it makes on him, through his eyes. But others—Ronald Peacock, for example—insist that society's demands are justified. The key figure of Antonio presents contradictory aspects, some positive and some negative. Some critics have sought to explain these unresolved dissonances—as they see them—by reference to the genesis of the play: Antonio is an amalgam of two figures from different sources used by Goethe. But the play can also be seen as examining—not necessarily from any definitive viewpoint—different possible relationships between the artist and society. In earlier ages the artist was an integrated member of society, who did not question its values nor his own role as its servant. But the modern artist is more likely to be conscious of his own individuality (cf. above, p. 19 ff.), to question society's values and to become alienated from the social order and even from his fellow men.

3. The role of woman

Charlotte von Stein seems in some sense to be the model for
Goethe's characterization of Iphigenie and of the Princess
in *Tasso*. It is also sometimes suggested that these figures
represent Goethe's particular ideal of womanhood, at least at
this period of his life. In *Iphigenie* repeated reference is made
to the heroine's sex, and it may be that Iphigenie's successful
execution of her moral task is in some way connected with it.

> THOAS: Aufs Ungehoffte war ich nicht bereitet;
> Doch sollt' ich's auch erwarten: wusst' ich nicht,
> Dass ich mit einem Weibe rechten ging?
> IPHIGENIE: Schilt nicht, o König, unser arm Geschlecht.
> Nicht herrlich wie die euern, aber nicht
> Unedel sind die Waffen eines Weibes.

> THOAS: I was not prepared for what ran counter to my hopes; but I
> should expect it: did I not know that I was going to argue with a
> woman? IPHIGENIE: Do not scold our poor sex, king. A woman's
> weapons are not glorious like yours, but they are not ignoble. (I, 3)

And in *Tasso* although Antonio, the practical man of action,
appears as Tasso's principal antagonist, the Princess is the
chief spokesman of the values of society, and claims to speak
for society specifically because she is a woman:

> Willst du genau erfahren, was sich ziemt,
> So frage nur bei edlen Frauen an.
> Denn ihnen ist am meisten dran gelegen,
> Dass alles wohl sich zieme, was geschieht.
> ... Und wirst du die Geschlechter beide fragen:
> Nach Freiheit strebt der Mann, das Weib nach Sitte.

> If you want to find out exactly what is fitting, you need only ask noble
> ladies. For they are more concerned than others that everything
> that happens should be fitting.... And if you ask both sexes: man
> strives for freedom, woman for moral order. (II, 1)

As we read these lines, we remember the importance of 'Freiheit' to the younger Goethe.

4. Dramatic form

Both plays show in contrast to the earlier ones a concentration and an aspiration to a clarity and concision of form which one can call classical. Each has a cast of five, consisting of the protagonist and four others grouped symmetrically about him or her. Only Arkas in *Iphigenie* could be considered a minor character, with no specific significance of his own. The deployment of the characters on the stage in the two plays is very similar—notably, the disposition of the fourth act is exactly the same in both, with monologues of the protagonist alternating with dialogue scenes. Professor Peacock argues, however, that the classical form is only superficial: in fact *Iphigenie* and *Tasso* are, he says, characteristically 'loose and episodic' in construction. (*Goethe's Major Plays*, p. 24.)

Both plays are, of course, in verse, but in a medium new to Goethe's dramatic work: unrhymed iambic pentameter or *blank verse*, the traditional form of dramatic verse in England since the days of Shakespeare. This English verse-form seemed to suit German much better than the French alexandrine had done. In *Iphigenie* the blank verse grew naturally out of the prose of the first version of 1779, which has already a pervading iambic rhythm. One can similarly find iambic passages in the later scenes of *Egmont*. Lessing had chosen blank verse as the medium for his *Nathan der Weise* in 1779: this is the first important instance of the metre in German, although it had been tried before in the 1750's. Between them, *Nathan*, *Iphigenie* and Schiller's *Don Carlos* (1786) established blank verse as the 'classical' medium for serious drama in German.

4

The Classical Goethe: 1786–1806

A. General characterization

1. Italy

At the beginning of September 1786, Goethe was at Karlsbad
(now Karlovy Vary, in Czechoslovakia). On 3 September,
without returning to Weimar, he left for Italy. He arrived in
Venice on 28 September and in Rome on 29 October. In the
spring and early summer of 1787 he travelled south as far as
Sicily, then returned to Rome, where he remained until April
1788. In June of that year he arrived back in Weimar. Italy
had been not only the satisfaction of a long-felt yearning, but a
revelation as well. It was a land of light and clarity, in contrast
to the dark and gloom of northern Europe; and it accordingly
represented the possibility of new, objective forms of creation
in contrast to what now appeared to him as the subjectivity of
his earlier works:

> O wie fühl' ich in Rom mich so froh! gedenk' ich der
> Zeiten,
> Da mich ein graulicher Tag hinten im Norden umfing,
> Trübe der Himmel und schwer auf meine Scheitel sich
> senkte,
> Farb- und gestaltlos die Welt um den Ermatteten lag,
> Und ich uber mein Ich, des unbefriedigten Geistes
> Düstre Wege zu spähn, still in Betrachtung versank.
> Nun umleuchtet der Glanz des helleren Äthers die Stirne;
> Phöbus rufet, der Gott, Formen und Farben hervor.

O how happy I am to be in Rome! when I think of the times when a gloomy light enveloped me, back there in the north, where the sky sank dull and heavy upon my head, colourless and shapeless the world lay about me in my exhaustion, and I sank silently into contemplation of my own self, to spy out the dark ways of my dissatisfied spirit. Now the glow of a brighter ether shines about my forehead; Phoebus, the god, calls forth forms and colours. (*Römische Elegien*, No. 7, ll. 1–8)

Moreover, modern Italy seemed to keep alive the traditions of Roman antiquity, as Goethe now came to see them: a full and balanced life in which a healthy sensuality played its part, a harmony of intellect and senses, of art and life. In celebrating the Italian experience, and in reviving the metres of Latin poetry, the hexameter and the elegiac distich, Goethe is seeking to recreate this classical synthesis. The fifth of the *Roman Elegies* sums up all these themes.

> Froh empfind' ich mich nun auf klassischem Boden begeistert,
> > Vor- und Mitwelt spricht lauter and reizender mir.
> Hier befolg' ich den Rat, durchblättre die Werke der Alten
> > Mit geschäftiger Hand, täglich mit neuem Genuss.
> Aber die Nächte hindurch hält Amor mich anders beschäftigt;
> > Werd' ich auch halb nur gelehrt, bin ich doch doppelt beglückt.
> Und belehr' ich mich nicht, indem ich des lieblichen Busens
> > Formen spähe, die Hand leite die Hüften hinab?
> Dann versteh' ich den Marmor erst recht: ich denk' und vergleiche,
> > Sehe mit fühlendem Aug', fühle mit sehender Hand.
> Raubt die Liebste denn gleich mir einige Stunden des Tages,
> > Gibt sie Stunden der Nacht mir zur Entschädigung hin.
> Wird doch nicht immer geküsst, es wird vernünftig gesprochen;
> > Überfällt sie der Schlaf, lieg' ich und denke mir viel.

Oftmals hab' ich auch schon in ihren Armen gedichtet
  Und des Hexameters Mass leise mit fingernder Hand
Ihr auf den Rücken gezählt. Sie atmet in lieblichem
    Schlummer,
  Und es durchglühet ihr Hauch mir bis ins Tiefste die
    Brust.
Amor schüret die Lamp' indes und denket der Zeiten,
  Da er den nämlichen Dienst seinen Triumvirn getan.

Now on classical soil I find myself fired with joyous enthusiasm, past and present speak more loudly and urgently to me. Here I take the ancients' good advice, leaf through their works with busy hand, finding new pleasure every day. But during the night Cupid keeps me otherwise occupied; even if I only become half a scholar, my happiness is doubled. And am I not engaged in learning when I am scanning the forms of the delightful bosom, drawing my hand along the line of the hips? Only then do I really understand the marble statues; I think and compare, see with feeling eye and feel with seeing hand. And even if my mistress does rob me of some of the hours of daylight, she surrenders hours of the night for my compensation. And we do not only kiss, we have intelligent conversations; when sleep overcomes her, I lie awake and think many thoughts. Often I have composed poetry in her arms and gently counted out the measure of my hexameters on her back with the fingers of my hand. She breathes gently in her sleep, and her breathing fills my whole breast with a glow. Meanwhile Cupid trims the lamp and thinks of the times when he did the same service for his triumvirate [i.e. Catullus, Tibullus and Propertius: cf. p. 65 below].

In 1790 Goethe travelled to Italy again, but got no further than Venice, and the experience seems to have been disillusioning. However, the classical ideal remained.

Das ist Italien, das ich verliess. Noch stäuben die Wege,
  Noch ist der Fremde geprellt, stell' er sich, wie er auch
    will.
Deutsche Redlichkeit suchst du in allen Winkeln vergebens;
  Leben und Weben ist hier, aber nicht Ordnung und
    Zucht;
Jeder sorgt nur für sich, misstrauet dem andern, ist eitel,
  Und die Meister des Staats sorgen nur wieder für sich.

Schön ist das Land! doch ach, Faustinen find' ich nicht
wieder.
Das ist Italien nicht mehr, das ich mit Schmerzen verliess.

This is Italy, just as I left it. The roads are still dusty. They still cheat
the stranger, however he tries to defend himself. German honesty
you will look for in vain hereabouts; there is life and activity, but not
order or discipline; everyone looks after himself alone, mistrusts his
neighbour, is vain, and the great men of the state just look after themselves too. The country is beautiful! but alas, I cannot find Faustina
[the fictitious name of Goethe's (fictitious?) Roman mistress] again.
This is not the Italy I left with such sorrow. (*Venezianische Epigramme*,
No. 4).

2. Nature and science

Goethe's 'classical' period is the high point in his scientific
career. It was in Italy that his morphological theories, of plant
and animal metamorphosis, were formulated, and in Italy too
that he began the optical investigations, designed to disprove
Newton's theory of colours, which he was to pursue obsessively
for the rest of his life. Goethe's scientific theories and the attitude to nature underlying them can be called 'classical' in that
they reveal a classical belief in an ordered universe and a
classical concern for the unity of intellect and senses. Nature
manifests unity in diversity, permanence in change. The chief
driving forces in nature Goethe identified as 'Polarität'
('polarization') and 'Steigerung' ('heightening' or 'intensifica-
tion')—a dialectical interplay of opposites. These ideas are of
relevance to all life, and so we find them reflected in his other
writings. In scientific method Goethe was opposed to mathematical analysis, 'Trennen und Zählen' ('taking to pieces and
counting'). He believed that the mathematical scientists had
lost sight of the actual phenomena of nature. Thus to him
Newton's doctrine that white light is composed of the seven
prismatic colours of the spectrum was a blasphemous absur-
dity, for he regarded the opposition of light and darkness as a
primary phenomenon ('Urphänomen') which could not be

broken down. The experience of seeing rests on a pre-established harmony between the eye and light.

> Das Auge hat sein Dasein dem Licht zu danken. Aus gleichgültigen tierischen Hülfsorganen ruft sich das Licht ein Organ hervor, das seinesgleichen werde, und so bildet sich das Auge am Lichte fürs Licht, damit das innere Licht dem äusseren entgegentrete.

> The eye owes its existence to light. From among the random auxiliary organs of animals light calls forth an organ that shall be like itself, and so the eye by the agency of light is formed for the light, that the inner light may go to meet the outer. (Introduction to the *Farbenlehre* [*Theory of Colours*], written 1807)

This passage has a mystico-religious ring. So too have the words addressed to Chancellor von Müller in May 1828[1] in which Goethe briefly recalls the scientific intuitions of the Italian journey:

> Die Versatilität der Natur in Pflanzenreiche verfolgte ich unablässig und es glückte mir Anno 1787 in Sizilien die Metamorphose der Pflanzen, so im Anschauen wie im Begriff, zu gewinnen. Die Metamorphose des Tierreichs lag nahe dran und im Jahre 1790 offenbarte sich mir in Venedig der Ursprung des Schädels aus Wirbelknochen . . .

> Unceasingly I investigated the versatile forms shown by nature in the vegetable kingdom, and in the year 1787 in Sicily I succeeded in gaining an intuition, as well as a concept, of the metamorphosis of plants. The next thing was the metamorphosis of the animal kingdom, and in the year 1790 in Venice the formation of the skull from vertebrae revealed itself to me. . . .

The word 'Anschauen', which philosophers normally trans-

---

[1] An explanatory note to an essay on Nature, dating from 1783, which had been wrongly attributed to Goethe. *HA* vol. 13, p. 48 f. It is also in this note that Goethe expounds to Müller the doctrine of 'Polarität' and 'Steigerung' mentioned above.

late 'intuition', means of course literally 'looking at': 'vision' would perhaps be a better English equivalent. Goethe continually emphasizes that one must *see* the phenomena of nature ('schauen') and *enjoy* them ('sich freuen,' 'erfreuen'), not merely construct fanciful theories about them ('schwärmen'). And this applies to the whole of life.

> Dieser schöne Begriff von Macht und Schranken, von Willkür
> Und Gesetz, von Freiheit und Mass, von beweglicher Ordnung,
> Vorzug und Mangel erfreue dich hoch! Die heilige Muse
> Bringt harmonisch ihn dir, mit sanftem Zwange belehrend.
> Keinen höhern Begriff erringt der sittliche Denker,
> Keinen der tätige Mann, der dichtende Künstler; der Herrscher,
> Der verdient, es zu sein, erfreut nur durch ihn sich der Krone.
> Freue dich, höchstes Geschöpf, der Natur! Du fühlest dich fähig,
> Ihr den höchsten Gedanken, zu dem sie schaffend sich aufschwang,
> Nachzudenken. Hier stehe nun still und wende die Blicke
> Rückwarts, prüfe, vergleiche und nimm vom Munde der Muse,
> Dass du schauest, nicht schwärmst, die liebliche volle Gewissheit.

May this beautiful idea of power and limitations, of liberty and law, of freedom and measure, of flexible order, advantage here and lack there, be a great delight to you! The holy Muse brings it to you in harmonies, instructing you with gentle compulsion. The moral thinker attains to no higher idea, nor the man of action nor the poet; the ruler who deserves his position only enjoys his crown by virtue of this idea. Rejoice, highest of creatures,[1] in nature! You feel yourself capable of following her in the highest thoughts to which she rose in creation. Stand still now and look backwards, examine, compare and hear from the Muse's lips that you see, and do not merely imagine, this full delightful certainty. (*Metamorphose der Tiere*, concluding lines)

3. Revolution

Having now formed an image of a universe ordered according to a grand harmonious design, Goethe was firmly opposed to any attempts at violent disruption of existing order. At no time did he share the enthusiasm with which many of his contemporaries at least initially greeted the French Revolution. Many years later he declared that

> Es ist besser, dass Ungerechtigkeiten geschehen, als dass sie auf eine ungerechte Weise gehoben werden.

> It is better that injustices should occur, than that they should be removed in an unjust way. (*Maximen und Reflexionen*)

and in the *Campagne in Frankreich*, his retrospective account of the counter-revolutionary campaign of 1792, he records in detail his distaste for the spread of democratic ideas. In a number of poetic works of the 1790s too he takes issue with the Revolution and what it stood for. Civil disturbance is directly portrayed in a number of plays, and the epics *Reineke Fuchs* (*Reynard the Fox*, 1793) and *Hermann und Dorothea* (1796–7) are, respectively, a satirical portrayal of a chaotic world and an idealized portrait of the forces of stability. The betrothal of Hermann and Dorothea with which the latter poem ends is the building of a symbolic bulwark against the forces of revolution and disintegration.

> Aber der Bräutigam sprach mit edler, männlicher Rührung:
> „Desto fester sei bei der allgemeinen Erschüttrung,
> Dorothea, der Bund! Wir wollen halten und dauern,

---

[1] In the German, as in my translation, the removal of this comma gives a different sense. Either reading can be justified: Goethe's MS. has no comma, but editions published in his lifetime have it.

Fest uns halten und fest der schönen Güter Besitztum.

Denn der Mensch, der zur schwankenden Zeit auch
schwankend gesinnt ist,

Der vermehret das Übel und breitet es weiter und weiter;

Aber wer fest auf dem Sinne beharrt, der bildet die Welt
sich.

Nicht dem Deutschen geziemt es, die fürchterliche
Bewegung

Fortzuleiten und auch zu wanken hierhin und dorthin.

‚Dies ist unser!' so lass uns sagen und so es behaupten!"

But her fiancé spoke with noble, manly emotion: 'In this time of
general commotion, Dorothea, let our bond be all the firmer! We
are going to hold and to last, to hold fast to each other and to our
fine possessions. For the man who in an unstable age is also unstable
in his mind, increases the evil and causes it to spread more and more;
but the man who is firm in his own mind forms the world about him.
It is not fitting for the German to carry on this fearful agitation and to
vacillate this way and that. "This is ours!" let us say, and be firm
in this!' (Canto IX, ll. 298–307)

4. Friendship with Schiller

Friedrich Schiller was ten years younger than Goethe. On his
return from Italy Goethe looked with disfavour on the young
revolutionary and author of *Die Räuber* (*The Robbers*, 1781),
one of the wildest of all 'Sturm und Drang' plays—at least,
that is how Goethe saw it. But Schiller himself in *Don Carlos*,
completed in 1786, had turned to blank verse drama in a more
'classical' style, and since then had devoted himself to the
study of history, Kantian philosophy, and aesthetics. In 1794,
after one or two previous, unfruitful meetings, their friendship
began. The ice was broken by Schiller in a letter of 13 June,
inviting Goethe to contribute to his periodical *Die Horen*.
On 23 August Schiller addressed to Goethe a remarkable letter
in which, as Goethe says in his reply, Schiller 'summed up his
whole being' ('die Summe meiner Existenz ziehen') and struck
a note with which the classical Goethe could immediately
sympathize:

c

Wären Sie als ein Grieche, ja nur als ein Italiener geboren worden, und hätte schon von der Wiege an eine auserlesene Natur und eine idealisierende Kunst Sie umgeben, so wäre Ihr Weg unendlich verkürzt, vielleicht ganz überflüssig gemacht worden. Schon in die erste Anschauung der Dinge hätten Sie dann die Form des Notwendigen aufgenommen, und mit Ihren ersten Erfahrungen hätte sich der grosse Stil in Ihnen entwickelt. Nun, da Sie ein Deutscher geboren sind, da Ihr griechischer Geist in diese nordische Schöpfung geworfen wurde, so blieb Ihnen keine andere Wahl, als entweder selbst zum nordischen Künstler zu werden, oder Ihrer Imagination das, was ihr die Wirklichkeit vorenthielt, durch Nachhilfe der Denkkraft zu ersetzen und so gleichsam von innen heraus und auf einem rationalen Wege ein Griechenland zu gebären.

If you had been born a Greek, or even an Italian, and if from your cradle you had been surrounded by the finest forms of nature and an idealizing art, then your journey would have been made infinitely shorter, perhaps altogether superfluous. Even your first intuitions of things would have been informed by a sense of their necessary essences, and with your first experience the high style would have developed within you. Now, since you were born a German, since your Greek spirit was cast into this Nordic world, you had no other choice than that of either becoming a Nordic artist yourself, or of supplying your imagination, by an effort of the conscious mind, with those things reality denied to it, and thus as it were giving birth to a Greece of your own, from within yourself and by the methods of reason.

Until Schiller's death in May 1805 the two collaborated in the attempt to 'give birth to a Greece of their own', through the establishment of a permanently valid literary theory and the production of exemplary 'objective' and 'classical' works. Yet Schiller also encouraged Goethe to complete two works which are in the one case doubtfully, in the other not at all 'classical' in form, but which are nevertheless the most important large-scale products of these years: the novel *Wilhelm Meisters Lehr-*

jahre (*Wilhelm Meister's Apprenticeship*), completed in 1796, and the First Part of *Faust*, finished in 1806.

B. Poetry

In the periods of Goethe's creative life with which we have been concerned hitherto, content and expressive power have been of paramount importance in his poetry, and the great variety of forms with which we have observed him experimenting is subordinate to these purposes. At the height of Goethe's classicism, however, form assumes great importance for its own sake; specifically, we find him writing the bulk of his poetry during these years in metres imitated from Greek and Latin verse. It will therefore be convenient to divide the poetry of the classical period into two broad categories on a formal basis: poems in classical metres, and lyrics and ballads in other forms. It will also be necessary to go into some technical detail.

1. Classical metres
These had been used by German poets before Goethe, notably by Klopstock (cf. p. 9 above) and Voss. Klopstock, and later Hölderlin in his odes of the 1790s, used a variety of Classical strophic forms as well as the comparatively simple hexameter and elegiac distich. Goethe used the iambic trimeter of Greek tragedy in the 'Helen' act of *Faust II* (see p. 114 below) and one or two other dramatic metres in fragments which remained unfinished; otherwise he confined himself to hexameters and elegiacs.

Critical opinion has always been divided on the success of Goethe's use of these metres, though the *Römische Elegien* and *Hermann und Dorothea* are generally agreed to be among his masterpieces. The burden of adverse criticism is that it is 'artificial' to attempt to use these metres in German, since they originated in languages whose versification was based upon a completely different principle. Greek and Latin metres were based upon the measurement of long and short syllables, the natural accentuation or stress of the words being largely if not entirely disregarded. In German versification, however, accentuation is, as in English, of great importance; in some metres the *number* of syllables is significant, but the notion of syllable *length* has little if any meaning. Goethe's classical lines should be read like any other German poetry: that is, the normal accentuation of the words should not be excessively distorted. All verse necessarily involves some such distortion, or it would not be verse: the rhythm of the words is made to conform to a pattern. This is true even of free verse, the only difference being that there the pattern is irregular. All that is 'artificial' about classical metres is that the pattern is clearly defined, and unfamiliar.

(*a*) *Hexameters.* As its name indicates, the hexameter is a line of six metrical units. In Greek and Latin it is a line of six 'feet', which may be 'spondees' (consisting of two long syllables, conventionally notated — —), or 'dactyls' (consisting of one long syllable followed by two short ones, notated — ∪ ∪). Dactyls and spondees are used in free alternation, except that the last two feet are (almost) invariably a dactyl followed by a spondee:

$$— ∪ ∪ \ \Big| \ — ∪ ∪ \ \Big| \ — ∪ ∪ \ \Big| \ — ∪ ∪ \ \Big| \ — ∪ ∪ \ \Big| \ — —$$
$$— — \ \ \ \ \Big| \ — — \ \ \Big| \ — — \ \ \Big| \ — — \ \ \ \ \ \Big|$$

It will be noted that the *number* of syllables in the line may vary from 13 to 17.

The German hexameter is a line with six *accents* or stresses. It too may vary from 13 syllables to 17 in length, from

In dás Haus díe Braut mít schöner Mítgift heréinführst

Bring your bride home with a fine dowry. (*Hermann und Dorothea*, II, 170)

to

´   x x   ´ x   x   ´ x   x ´ x   x ´ x   x ´   x
Aber ich sehe schon, Lügen bedarf es, und über die Massen

But I can see I shall have to tell lies, and plenty of them. (*Reineke Fuchs*, IV, 276)

The variation in the number of *unstressed* syllables (indicated here by x's) gives the German hexameter a somewhat elusive rhythm. This elusiveness, however, is part of the character of the line, and not necessarily evidence of 'artificiality'. An important feature is that the line always begins with a stressed syllable, with no 'Auftakt' ('up-beat' or 'anacrusis'): the verse always has 'falling rhythm' (whereas blank verse, for example, regularly has 'rising rhythm'). But even this clear characteristic can be blurred by *enjambement*, or running the sense on from one line to the next, this making the rhythm still more elusive:

´   x   ´ x x ´ x   x ´   x   ´ x x   ´ x
Wagt ihr, also bereitet, die letzte Stufe zu steigen
´ x   ´   x   x ´   x x   ´   x   ´   x x   ´ x
Dieses Gipfels, so reicht mir die Hand und öffnet den freien
´   x   ´ x ´   x   x ´
Blick ins weite Feld der Natur . . .

If, thus prepared, you are bold enough to climb the last pinnacle of this mountain-top, then give me your hand and cast your unobstructed gaze upon the wide realm of nature. . . . (*Metamorphose der Tiere*, ll. 1–3)

This is almost prose; but in addition to its clarity and even flow, the virtually concealed rhythmic regularity gives it a subtle elegance.

In Greek and Latin the hexameter is an *epic* metre, i.e. one employed for long narrative or expository poems, and Goethe uses it accordingly. The three major works in this metre are, however, very different in character. *Reineke Fuchs* (*Reynard the Fox*), portraying the exploits of the cunning fox who ultimately gets the better of all other animals, is satirical, racy, often even scurrilous in tone. *Hermann und Dorothea* opposes to this chaotic vision an idealization of simple country life and of the virtues of the German character. The story is told in a series of stylized tableaux. The mannerisms of classical epic poetry are deliberately imitated to give the work an antique flavour: the laudatory epithets—often placed after the noun: 'das Land, das schöne' ('the land, the beautiful', I. 10)—the elaborate yet generalized descriptions, the participial constructions and deliberate distortion of normal prose word-order, the rhetorical formulae with which speakers are introduced:

> Sorgsam brachte die Mutter des klaren, herrlichen Weines
> In geschliffener Flasche auf blankem, zinnernem Runde,
> Mit den grünlichen Römern, den echten Bechern des Rheinweins.
> Und so sitzend, umgaben die drei den glänzend gebohnten,
> Runden, braunen Tisch, er stand auf mächtigen Füssen.
> Heiter klangen sogleich die Gläser des Wirtes und Pfarrers;
> Doch unbeweglich hielt der Dritte denkend das seine,
> Und es fordert' ihn auf der Wirt mit freundlichen Worten:

> Carefully the mother brought of the clear, splendid wine in cut glass decanters on polished pewter disc, with the greenish goblets, the true glasses of Rhine wine. And thus sitting, the three surrounded the gleamingly polished, round, brown table, it stood on sturdy feet. Cheerfully sounded straightway the glasses of the landlord and the pastor; but motionless the third pensively held his, and the landlord called on him with friendly words ... (Canto I, ll. 166–173)

Finally, the *Metamorphose der Tiere* (*Metamorphosis of Animals*) is a fragment of an intended didactic epic on the whole of nature, after such classical models as Lucretius' *De Rerum Natura*.

(*b*) *Elegiacs*. The elegiac distich consists of a hexameter followed by a pentameter. Schiller's paradigm is often quoted:

> Im Hexameter steigt des Springquells flüssige Säule,
> Im Pentameter drauf fällt sie melodisch herab.

In the hexameter rises the fountain's silvery column,
In the pentameter aye falling in melody back. (Coleridge)

The pentameter is misleadingly named (at least as far as German prosody is concerned) because it is a line of *six* stresses, not five. It consists in theory of two half-hexameters, equalling twice two-and-a-half feet.

  ´ x ´ x x   ´ ´   x   x ´ x   x ´
  Im Pentameter drauf fällt sie melodisch herab
(theoretical scheme:

— — | — ∪ ∪ | — ‖ — ∪ ∪ | — ∪ ∪ | —)

The pentameter (which is not used by itself, but only in the elegiac distich) has from the German point of view a very unusual shape. The juxtaposition of two stressed syllables, which in ordinary German verse forms only occurs as an irregularity or syncopation, is here a regular feature.

  ´   x x ´ x x   ´ ´   x x   x x ´
  Erst die Orange, die schwer ruht, als ein goldener Ball
  (*Alexis und Dora*, l. 86)

An English pentameter equivalent would be

  ´   x ´ x   x ´ ´ x   ´ x x ´
  First the orange, a ball, firm and heavy, of gold.

The elegiac distich is thus heavily weighted with stresses and pauses. This gives it its rising-and-falling character, as Schiller called it, quite unlike the even flow of hexameter verse.

An *elegy*, in classical terminology, is a longer poem in this metre. It may have what we customarily call 'elegiac', that is, sad or reflective character: such is Goethe's *Euphrosyne*, a poem on the death of the actress Christiane Neumann. But it is not necessarily so. In the *Römische Elegien* (*Roman Elegies*) of 1788, originally entitled *Erotica Romana*, Goethe is following the tradition of Catullus, Tibullus and Propertius (cf. No. 5, p. 54 above), using the form for love poetry, celebrating both

the Italian experience and his own imitation of uninhibited
Classical sensuality in his liaison with Christiane Vulpius (cf.
above, p. 5); and the *Metamorphose der Pflanzen* (*Metamorphosis of Plants*) is both a love-poem for Christiane and a
didactic poem expounding Goethe's doctrines of nature. A
shorter poem in this metre is called an *epigram*. This often consists of a single distich; some of the *Venezianische Epigramme*
(*Venetian Epigrams*), however, are exceptionally long, running
to a dozen lines or more.

2. Poetry in other forms

Side by side with the classical forms we find a variety of others.
The dithyrambic free verse of the earlier hymnic poetry (cf.
p. 19 ff. above) has disappeared, but Goethe experiments with a
number of metres and strophic forms, rhymed and unrhymed.
Of this poetry, comparatively little is of immediate personal
content. It is, generally speaking, objective, and so is itself in a
sense classical, although Goethe is not using antique metres.
Thus form is here too a consideration of great importance,
even when the content is quintessentially Goethean.

(*a*) *Ballads and sonnets.* In 1797 Goethe and Schiller discussed
the aesthetic character of the ballad and set themselves the
task of writing poems in this form. While for Herder (cf. p. 15 f.
above) the 'primitive' character of the ballad had been a wholly
positive quality, for Goethe and Schiller at the height of their
classicism it meant that the form could not—or need not—be
taken entirely seriously: both regarded the ballads of 1797 as
something of a relaxation from higher things. Nevertheless,
precisely from the formal point of view Goethe's contributions
are of great interest, each one being in a different form.
The characteristic theme of these ballads is the encounter between man and supernatural powers: a god in *Der Gott und die
Bajadere* (*The God and the Dancing-girl*), a vampire in *Die
Braut von Korinth* (*The Bride of Corinth*), witchcraft in *Der
Zauberlehrling* (*The Wizard's Apprentice*). But Goethe is not so

much concerned here, as in *Erlkönig* (p. 40 f. above), with the menace of the supernatural in itself, but with the correct balance between man and the other, superhuman elements in the universe of which he too forms an integral part. *Legende* (*Legend*) treats the theme of the appearance of the divine in everyday life in a simple, homely, humorous way, choosing for this the old-fashioned *Knittelvers*:

> Als noch, verkannt und sehr gering,
> Unser Herr auf der Erde ging,
> Und viele Jünger sich zu ihm fanden,
> Die sehr selten sein Wort verstanden,
> Liebt' er sich gar über die Massen,
> Seinen Hof zu halten auf der Strassen,
> Weil unter des Himmels Angesicht
> Man immer besser und freier spricht.

When, unrecognized and very humble, our Lord walked the earth, and many disciples joined him who very rarely understood what he was saying, he had a great liking for holding court out in the street, because under the face of heaven one always speaks better and more freely. (ll. 1–8).

Another group, or rather two groups, of poems from the later part of Goethe's classical period deserve mention from the point of view of form: the sonnets. The sonnet form was extremely popular with German poets of the seventeenth century, suffered almost complete eclipse in the eighteenth and was then revived by the Romantics. Goethe's two sonnets of about 1800, *Das Sonett* (*The Sonnet*) and *Natur und Kunst* (*Nature and Art*) allude to the Romantic challenge, but also define the nature of the sonnet. This, although it is not an antique form (and despite its attraction for the Romantics), is in a sense a classical one, in that the poet must, in the words of the first sonnet,

... dich ... bestimmt bewegen
Nach Tritt und Schritt, wie es dir vorgeschrieben.

... move in the prescribed way, by step and pace, as it is laid down
for you. (ll. 3–4)

And the second sonnet concludes with a *credo* of the classical
Goethe:

In der Beschränkung zeigt sich erst der Meister,
Und das Gesetz nur kann uns Freiheit geben.

Only in limitation can the master begin to show himself and only law
can give us freedom.

The second group of sonnets is a sequence of seventeen,
written in 1807–8: on these see p. 93 f. below.

(*b*) '*Gott und Welt*.' A number of poems from the classical
phase of his life were grouped by Goethe together with others
of later date, in the definitive edition of his works (*Ausgabe
letzter Hand*) which appeared in 1827, under the title *Gott und
Welt* (*God and the World*). The group includes the two 'Metamorphosis' poems, *Dauer und Wechsel* (*Permanence and Change*)
and *Weltseele* (*World-Soul*). With these poems Goethe continues the line of the earlier hymns, defining the nature of the
divine and the relationship of man to it. The two ballads
Der Gott und die Bajadere and *Die Braut von Korinth* should also
be considered in this connexion. Both are, in a sense, religious
poems, though *Die Braut von Korinth* is explicitly anti-Christian
in tendency and the moral of *Der Gott und die Bajadere* is by
no means as orthodox as it may appear when quoted by itself:

Es freut sich die Gottheit der reuigen Sünder;
Unsterbliche heben verlorene Kinder
Mit feurigen Armen zum Himmel empor.

The godhead rejoices over repentant sinners; immortals raise fallen
children to heaven with fiery arms. (ll. 97–9)

Poems such as these give us an intimation of the ironical style of Goethe's later years.

C. The novel

In his first years at Weimar (or possibly, it has been argued, even earlier), Goethe had begun work on a novel to be entitled *Wilhelm Meisters theatralische Sendung* (*Wilhelm Meister's Theatrical Mission*). By 1786 he had completed six books of this, but the work was then allowed to lapse; and when Goethe took it up again in 1794 he changed it into something radically different in form and purport. *Wilhelm Meisters Lehrjahre* (*Wilhelm Meister's Apprenticeship*), as it was now called, in eight books—its first four corresponding roughly to the six completed books of the *Sendung*—was completed in 1796. A manuscript copy of the *Sendung* was discovered in 1910, and the two versions can now be compared. It has been observed that the *Sendung* is more vivid, more realistic, more immediate in its impact than the *Lehrjahre*; but it should be remembered that as far as Goethe's own intentions are concerned, the later version completely supplanted the earlier one.

Goethe produced one other work of prose fiction at this time: the *Unterhaltungen deutscher Ausgewanderten* (*Conversations of German Émigrés*, 1795) a cycle of short stories presented in the fictional framework of conversations between a group of German aristocrats, forced by the advancing armies of revolutionary France to flee from their property on the left bank of the Rhine. This is a minor work, but of some historical significance both for the development of the German 'Novelle' as a whole and for the technique of Goethe's own later novels, which make increasing use of interpolated 'Novellen'. The story of most intrinsic interest in the *Unterhaltungen* is the *Märchen* or fairy-tale with which the cycle concludes: a blend of magic, alchemy, freemasonry and pure fancy, designed, as its narrator tells his listeners, to remind us of 'alles und nichts'—

of everything and of nothing at all. This too, although appearing in Goethe's classical phase (albeit before the collaboration with Schiller was really under way) is profoundly unclassical in character.

WILHELM MEISTER

1. The theatre

Wilhelm's first ambition is to be the founder of a German national theatre: a topical aim, which Lessing among others had set himself, and which Goethe and Schiller themselves were now attempting—in a different way, under Court patronage—in Weimar. The novel contains vivid portraits of the different forms and changing tastes of the German theatre in the 1770's. Wilhelm's aspiration is partly a genuine ideal, partly however motivated by sheer escapism and partly by the fact that he is in love with an actress:

> Er glaubte den hellen Wink des Schicksals zu verstehen, das ihm durch Marianen die Hand reichte, sich aus dem stockenden, schleppenden bürgerlichen Leben herauszureissen, aus dem er schon so lange sich zu retten gewünscht hatte. Seines Vaters Haus, die Seinigen zu verlassen, schien ihm etwas Leichtes. Er war jung und neu in der Welt, und sein Mut, in ihren Weiten nach Glück und Befriedigung zu rennen, durch die Liebe erhöht. Seine Bestimmung zum Theater war ihm nunmehr klar; das hohe Ziel, das er sich vorgesteckt sah, schien ihm näher, indem er an Marianens Hand hinstrebte, und in selbstgefälliger Bescheidenheit erblickte er in sich den trefflichen Schauspieler, den Schöpfer eines künftigen Nationaltheaters, nach dem er so vielfältig hatte seufzen hören.

He thought he had received a clear hint from destiny, which had stretched out its hand to him in the person of Mariane, to tear himself free from sluggish, hesitant everyday life, from which he had so long yearned to be rescued. To leave his father's house and his family seemed an easy matter to him. He was young and new to the world, and his keenness to run through the world in search of fortune and satisfaction was enhanced by love. His vocation to the theatre was now clear to him; the high goal he saw set before him seemed nearer when he strove at Mariane's side, and in no excess of modesty he saw in himself the superlative actor, the creator of a future National Theatre, that he had heard so many sigh for. (Book I, ch. 9)

The irony here is evident. It is a point of critical debate whether the earlier version of the novel, the *Sendung*, is similarly ironical: most critics have thought not, but a few have taken the ironical view. In the *Lehrjahre* it is clear that the theatre cannot satisfy Wilhelm, and he himself turns away from the theatre and gives up his supposed vocation. Yet the preponderance of irony may not wholly exclude a serious view of the theatre as a microcosm of society. When Wilhelm tells Jarno of his dissatisfaction with the theatre and his desire to give it up, Jarno replies:

> ,,Wissen Sie denn, mein Freund ... dass Sie nicht das Theater, sondern die Welt beschrieben haben ...?"

> 'Don't you know, my friend, that it isn't the theatre you have described to me, but the world?' (Book VII, ch. 3)

2. '*Bildung*'

The *Sendung* was a 'Theaterroman', a novel of the theatre, the *Lehrjahre* is a 'Bildungsroman', a novel portraying the education and development of an individual to his full potential, in accordance with the natural bent of his personality:

> ,,Dass ich Dir's mit *einem* Worte sage: Mich selbst, ganz wie ich da bin, auszubilden, das war dunkel von Jugend auf mein Wunsch und meine Absicht."

> 'To tell you in a single word: to educate myself, my whole self, that has been, indistinctly from my early days, my wish and my intention.' (Book V, ch. 3: Wilhelm's letter to Werner)

What 'Bildung' is *not* is clearly stated by Jarno:

> „Nicht allen Menschen ist es eigentlich um ihre Bildung
> zu tun; viele wünschen nur so ein Hausmittel zum Wohl-
> befinden, Rezepte zum Reichtum und zu jeder Art von
> Glückseligkeit. Alle diese [wollen] nicht auf ihre Füsse
> gestellt sein . . .“

'Not all men are really concerned to educate themselves; many only
desire a kind of patent medicine, or recipes for riches and for every
variety of happiness. All these people don't want to be set on their
own feet . . .' (Book VIII, ch. 5)

Wilhelm does want to be 'set on his own feet': clearly, however,
this will be a long and difficult process. The years of apprentice-
ship must (in accordance with German practice) be followed by
'Wanderjahre', 'years of travel', before the craftsman (whatever
his chosen trade or vocation) can justly call himself 'Meister'
('Master'). Later (cf. p. 100 below) Goethe duly provided
Wilhelm Meisters Lehrjahre with a sequel, *Wilhelm Meisters
Wanderjahre*. Here Wilhelm is characterized as follows:

> „Jetzt besonders,“ sagte Jarno, „seh' ich dich an wie einen
> Wanderstab, der die wunderliche Eigenschaft hat, in jeder
> Ecke zu grünen, wo man ihm hinstellt, nirgends aber
> Wurzel zu fassen . . .“

'Now in particular,' said Jarno, 'you seem to me like a traveller's staff,
with the miraculous property that it will put out leaves wherever
it is rested, but will not take root anywhere.' (*Wanderjahre*, Book I,
ch. 4)

The novel brings its hero into a variety of environments, and
thus becomes not merely the portrait of the growth and
development of an individual, but also of the society in which
he moves.

3. Society

Much of the novel is still concerned with the theatre. But the
theatre does in many ways serve as a microcosm of society.
The idea of a National Theatre was a focus for cultural aspirations in the German-speaking world in the eighteenth century.
After the attempt to establish a National Theatre at Hamburg
in the late sixties had failed, Lessing observed:

> Über den gutherzigen Einfall, den Deutschen ein National-
> theater zu verschaffen, da wir Deutsche noch keine Nation
> sind! Ich rede nicht von der politischen Verfassung, son-
> dern bloss von dem sittlichen Charakter.

> What is one to think of this well-meaning idea of creating a national
> theatre for the Germans, when we Germans are not yet a nation!
> I am not speaking of our political constitution, but only of our moral
> character. (*Hamburgische Dramaturgie*, Nos. 101–4)

The national theatre was to create the nation, rather than the
other way about. In a portrait of eighteenth-century German
society the theatre can legitimately occupy a major position.
But we are also shown other possibilities: the world of
business, represented by Werner; the withdrawal from society
into a private moral and religious world represented by the
'schöne Seele' ('beautiful soul') whose 'confessions' make up
the sixth book. But none of these possibilities does in fact solve
the twin problems of the development of the individual and of a
productive relationship between the individual and society.
Such solution seems to be possible, at any rate under the existing
social circumstances, for the nobleman.

> „Ich weiss nicht, wie es in fremden Ländern ist, aber in
> Deutschland ist nur dem Edelmann eine gewisse allge-
> meine, wenn ich sagen darf, personelle Ausbildung möglich.
> Ein Bürger kann sich Verdienst erwerben und zur höchsten
> Not seinen Geist ausbilden; seine Persönlichkeit geht aber

verloren, er mag sich stellen, wie er will . . . Er darf nicht fragen: ,Was bist du?', sondern nur: ,Was hast du? welche Einsicht, welche Kenntnis, welche Fähigkeit, wieviel Vermögen?' Wenn der Edelmann durch die Darstellung seiner Person alles gibt, so gibt der Bürger durch seine Persönlichkeit nichts und soll nichts geben . . . Jener soll tun und wirken, dieser soll leisten und schaffen; er soll einzelne Fähigkeiten ausbilden, um brauchbar zu werden, und es wird schon vorausgesetzt, dass in seinem Wesen keine Harmonie sei noch sein dürfe, weil er, um sich auf *eine* Weise brauchbar zu machen, alles übrige vernachlässigen muss."

'I do not know what it is like in other countries, but in Germany only the nobleman can achieve a certain general education of his person, so to speak. A man from the middle classes can gain recognition of his merit and at the very most, train his mind; but his personality suffers thereby, whatever he does. . . . He may not ask "What are you" but only "What have you got? What insight, what knowledge, what capacities, how much money?" Whereas the nobleman gives all he has merely by being himself, the ordinary citizen gives nothing by virtue of his mere personality, nor is it expected of him . . . the former is expected to be active and effectual, the latter only to be productive and to do his job; he has to train particular abilities in order to be of service, and it is already assumed that there neither is nor need be any harmony in his being, because he has, in order to make himself useful in one way, to neglect everything else.' (*Lehrjahre*, Book V, ch. 3: Wilhelm to Werner)

In the *Lehrjahre* Wilhelm is emancipated from his restricted, middle-class way of life, firstly by the theatre, then by admission to aristocratic society and to the classless, but in practice aristocratically-based, freemasonry of the 'Society of the Tower'. The *Wanderjahre* goes on to show how this society benefits mankind at large: in the later novel Goethe is much less concerned with individual 'Bildung'. (Cf. below, p. 104 f.)

4. Narrative technique

The *Lehrjahre* is not a realistic novel. The *Sendung* is more realistic: in the *Lehrjahre* Goethe's stylistic intentions have changed. He freely makes use of the devices of popular fiction in his plot, which is spun together from a journey, a number of love stories, and a mystery or two—the strange characters of the Harper and Mignon, and the mysterious interventions of the 'Society of the Tower'—with liberal use of coincidence and comparatively little concern for verisimilitude. This is intended to make it clear to the reader that the action is to be understood symbolically rather than literally—like the interconfessional family reunion at the end of Lessing's *Nathan der Weise*, or the Masonic imitations of Mozart's *Magic Flute* (1791). Similarly the progress of the action as such is less important than the stylized tableaux it frequently produces; this technique is also employed in *Hermann und Dorothea*.

D. Drama

In the drama, the major outcome of Goethe's classical period was the completion of works begun at an earlier date. *Iphigenie* was recast in verse soon after Goethe's arrival in Italy. *Egmont*, though it remains essentially a non-classical work, received its finishing touches in 1788, and *Tasso* was developed in Italy and completed in 1789. Also in Italy Goethe resumed work on *Faust*, which he had probably done little or nothing to since his arrival in Weimar. He hoped to complete it for the new edition of his works, but only a fragment could be published in 1790; *Faust* then once more lay dormant, but in 1797 he again set to work in earnest and Part I was completed in 1806.

There is, however, also a group of dramatic works which were both conceived and executed during the classical period. These deal directly with the French Revolution and what it stood for. But the comedies *Der Gross-Cophta* (*The Grand Copt*, 1791) and *Der Bürgergeneral* (*The Citizen General*, 1793) both written at great speed, are generally accounted failures, and *Die Aufgeregten* (*Agitation*, 1794) remained a fragment, although Goethe later averred, in a conversation with Eckermann on 4 January 1824, that it could 'to some extent be regarded as my political confession of faith at the time'. The austere symbolic drama *Die Natürliche Tochter* (*The Natural Daughter*, 1799–1803) which also portrays the disruption of an ordered society, is complete as such, but it was intended to be the first part of a never-completed trilogy and so is in a sense also a fragment. Its chief interest lies in its style, which is highly compressed and hyper-refined; it looks forward to elements of Goethe's later manner, and offers an extreme contrast to the very unclassical *Faust I*.

FAUST, PART I

1. Versions
Each of the three distinct stages of Goethe's work on *Faust I* is represented by a separate version of the text.

(*a*) *Urfaust.* Goethe had begun work on his Faust drama in the 1770s (cf. p. 25 f. above). By the time he went to Weimar, he had written a number of unconnected scenes and sketches in which appear the traditional figure of Faust and his traditional companions: Mephistopheles his familiar evil spirit, Wagner his 'famulus' or assistant, students in a Leipzig beer-cellar. He had also written the balladesque sequence of scenes forming the 'Gretchen tragedy': the story of a simple girl, seduced and abandoned—also a familiar theme of folk-song and a dramatic subject favoured by the 'Stürmer und Dränger' —cf. H. L. Wagner's *Die Kindsmörderin* (*The Infanticide*) and J. M. R. Lenz's *Die Soldaten* (*The Soldiers*), both of 1776— but forming no part of the traditional Faust legend. The extent of Goethe's early work on *Faust* is known to us from the so-called *Urfaust* or 'original *Faust*', a manuscript dating from approximately 1776 and discovered in 1887. The manuscript is not in Goethe's hand and was not intended for publication, though as in the case of the *Theatralische Sendung* (cf. p. 69) some critics have declared it to be in certain respects superior to the finished Part I; the *Urfaust* has even been performed, despite its fragmentary state.

(*b*) *Fragment*. In Italy Goethe wrote two new scenes: 'Hexenküche' ('Witch's Kitchen') in which Faust is rejuvenated by drinking a magic potion, and 'Wald und Höhle' ('Forest and Cave') in which he stands back from the course of the action and reflects upon it, until urged by Mephistopheles to return to Gretchen. These two new scenes, together with some of the *Urfaust* material incorporating a number of revisions of detail, appeared in the version published by Goethe in 1790 under the title *Faust, Ein Fragment*. There is still no clear shape to the work, and the end of the Gretchen episode is omitted, although we know from the *Urfaust* that it was already written: perhaps by this omission Goethe meant simply to emphasize that the work was still far from completion.

(*c*) *Part I*. In 1796, at the height of his classical period (and rather to Schiller's surprise) Goethe resumed work on *Faust*. The work grew and grew: Goethe added 350 lines of prefatory material—a dedicatory poem and two dramatic prologues, 'Vorspiel auf dem Theater' ('Prelude in the Theatre') and 'Prolog im Himmel' ('Prologue in Heaven'); a sequence of scenes totalling over a thousand lines of verse (ll. 602–1770) and serving to explain the appearance of Mephistopheles and the pact between him and Faust—the central feature of the Faust legend, but for Goethe the great, hitherto unsolved problem of the play; and another long scene, 'Walpurgisnacht' ('Walpurgis Night', the festival of witches) together with the following 'Intermezzo'. He also revised and rearranged some of the already extant material. The completed Part I was published in 1808.

In this final version, out of a total of 4,600 lines, just over a quarter represents material substantially unaltered since the 1770's: Faust's opening monologue, the conjuration of the 'Erdgeist' or Earth Spirit, and the subsequent conversation between Faust and Wagner; the comic, parodistic scene between Mephistopheles and the student; the drinking scene in 'Auerbachs Keller'; and the sequence of the Gretchen scenes, together with Faust's despairing final speech in the 'Wald und Höhle' scene and the brief prose scene 'Trüber Tag. Feld' ('Dull Day. Field'). There has been a certain amount of revision of this material, notably of the 'Auerbachs Keller' and the final prison scene ('Kerker'), both of which scenes are in prose in the *Urfaust* version.

Many of the editions of *Faust I* available to the student contain further details of the work's textual history, and the *Urfaust* and the *Fragment* of 1790 are also easily accessible.

2. The importance of the 'Entstehungsgeschichte'
The textual history of *Faust* is of importance for the light it may throw on the question of Goethe's intention and ultimately of the meaning of the work as a whole. There is an enormous range of critical opinion on these matters. One extreme view would be that Goethe knew exactly what he was doing all the time he was working on *Faust*, and that the completed work represents no more than the achievement of what he had intended in the 1770's. The other extreme view would be that Goethe had little or no over-all idea or consistent intention in *Faust* and merely found the figure of Faust (whatever may have attracted him to this figure in the first place) a sufficiently all-embracing symbol of human aspirations and human destiny —in accordance with Faust's words

> Und was der ganzen Menschheit zugeteilt ist
> Will ich in meinem innern Selbst geniessen,

> And the destiny allotted to the whole of humanity I desire to savour in my inner self (ll. 1770–1)—

to be allowed to stand as the central figure of a 'universal poem' embracing anything that Goethe happened to fancy, and grow-

ing higgledy-piggledy without any plan at all. The evidence
does not permit us to hold either view in its extreme form, but
it does allow very great disagreement. For the English student,
Eudo Mason's book, *Goethe's Faust, its Genesis and Purport*,
provides a guide to many of these controversies. Professor
Mason's own view is nearer to the first of our two extremes. He
holds that Goethe did have an overriding general idea, which
included from the very beginning the untraditional innovation
of Faust's salvation—on this point in particular there may well
be further disagreement—while recognizing that the execution
of this idea presented such difficulties that Goethe was forced
to change his plan. The great difficulty was, of course, the
introduction of Mephistopheles and the definition of his role.
Originally sent to Faust by the 'Erdgeist' or Spirit of Earth,
the restless spirit of amoral energy whom Faust conjures up
in the first scene, Mephisto becomes in the finished Part I, with
its Prologue in Heaven, an agent, an emissary almost, of the
Lord himself. But while this is obviously of central significance,
Mason persuasively argues that 'the great change in the plan of
Faust in 1797 was, in fact, fundamentally only a formal change,
a replacing of the originally contemplated complex of symbols
and myths with another more lucid, palpable and familiar one,
of a private mythology ... with the universally known
"mythology" of Christian tradition' (p. 273).

3. The principal characters

(*a*) *Faust.* It is not hard to see what attracted the youthful
Goethe to the figure of Faust: his surging discontent, his
boundless aspirations. These aspirations are later given the
generalized name of 'Streben' (striving)—a word which does
not occur in the *Urfaust* or in the *Fragment*, but is of considerable importance as a unifying concept in the finished work.

Es irrt der Mensch, solang' er strebt

('Man will err as long as he strives'), observes the Lord in the

'Prologue in Heaven'—implying that error arising out of striving does not necessarily lead to damnation. And Faust declares, as he signs his pact with Mephistopheles:

> Nur keine Furcht, dass ich dies Bündnis breche!
> Das Streben meiner ganzen Kraft
> Ist grade das, was ich verspreche.

Have no fear that I shall break this agreement! To strive with all my strength is just what I am promising. (l. 1741–3)

Of similar import and function is the term 'Tätigkeit' (activity), which is also used in the same way as a unifying concept in the *Lehrjahre*.

(*b*) *Gretchen*. That Gretchen was no part of the original Faust legend has already been pointed out (p. 26 above). Plainly the young Goethe felt that Faust, the seeker of experience, must not be denied this most quintessential of experiences, human love. That the connexion between the titanic Faust and the lover of Gretchen is not immediately clear has been argued by a number of critics. One might even infer, from the fact that Goethe found it necessary in the 1780's to have Faust (in the new scene 'Hexenküche') rejuvenated with a witch's aphrodisiac potion, that it was no longer as clear to Goethe himself as it had been. But the Gretchen tragedy is already complete, in its deliberately fragmentary style, in the *Urfaust*; and perhaps because of this, and because only as regards Gretchen does the action reach any conclusion within Part I—because in effect only the Gretchen tragedy provides any actual plot—the shape of Part I is still essentially determined by it, and Part I still seems at least as much a Gretchen as a Faust tragedy.

(*c*) *Mephistopheles*. In the *Urfaust*, Mephistopheles is the cynical schemer, often a very human devil: a number of Goethe's 'Sturm und Drang' acquaintances have been suggested as his model, including Herder himself, who could be a very sharp-tongued and destructive critic. Mephisto's cynicism is often amusing, though we are not allowed entirely to forget its brutal element. In the finished Part I he introduces himself as a nihilist, a believer in nothing:

> Ich bin der Geist, der stets verneint!
> Und das mit Recht; denn alles, was entsteht,
> Ist wert, dass es zugrunde geht;
> Drum besser wär's, dass nichts entstünde.

> I am the spirit who denies everything! And I am right; for everything that comes into being is fit only to be destroyed; so it would be better if nothing ever came into being. (ll. 1338–41)

Yet in the 'Prologue in Heaven' the Lord has already defined the function which this nihilism fulfils in the scheme of creation, in provoking man to positive effort.

> Des Menschen Tätigkeit kann allzuleicht erschlaffen,
> Er liebt sich bald die unbedingte Ruh;
> Drum geb' ich gern ihm den Gesellen zu,
> Der reizt und wirkt und muss als Teufel schaffen.

> Man's activity can all too easily slacken, he soon becomes fond of undisturbed rest; so I willingly give him the companion who provokes and influences, and who can only do this job as a devil. (ll. 340–3)

4. Style and form

Faust is stylistically a uniquely varied work. If it is possible to identify a basic metre, then it is the so-called 'madrigal verse', itself a varied form: the 'normal' line has four stresses, but longer and shorter lines are constantly introduced, and the rhyme scheme is similarly flexible. The metre can therefore respond immediately to any change in mood, or in order to mark a significant moment. But there is also free verse (in the scene with the 'Erdgeist', and in the so-called 'catechism scene' in which Faust expounds his pantheistic religious views to

Gretchen), blank verse (the opening monologue of the scene 'Wald und Höhle'), a variety of strophic forms, and a couple of scenes in prose. The range of expression is correspondingly great: colloquial, lyrical, cynical, sublime. In fact the whole emotional range of Goethe's poetry is to be found in *Faust*. In its deliberate adoption of this most unclassical diversity of form *Faust* is the most 'Shakespearian' of all Goethe's dramatic works.

During the phase of work which produced the *Fragment*, Goethe had evidently hoped to complete the work in one part. The *Fragment* itself does not exclude the possibility. Clearly, with the 'Gretchen tragedy' alone taking up about 1500 lines, such a work would have been of considerable size; for the Gretchen episode, however important it was to Goethe, can only be an episode in Faust's life. In accordance with the tradition (cf. Marlowe's version), Faust has to make his pact with the devil, rise to fame and glory, conjure up the shade of Helen of Troy, and meet his eventual end; and of all this the *Fragment* contains nothing. A work such as Schiller's *Maria Stuart* (4,033 lines) demonstrates that a long play need not necessarily be an unwieldy one; but Schiller's structure is based upon a firm plot, and quite unlike the episodic form of drama to which Goethe naturally inclined. At all events Goethe decided in or before 1797 that his *Faust* would have to be in two parts, and while completing Part I he was already working on Part II. Before they leave Faust's study, Mephistopheles tells Faust:

Wir sehn die kleine, dann die grosse Welt

We will see the little world, then the great world (Part I, l. 2052)

—giving us too a warning that there is a great deal more to come than the Gretchen episode. But like Part I, Part II was to grow in execution to something more than Goethe had at least consciously intended.

The Older Goethe, 1806–1832

A. General characteristics

1. Isolation and 'mysticism'
After Schiller's death and the completion of *Faust I*, Goethe became progressively more and more detached from the public and literary life of the day. His works become more wayward and individualistic—but not in the demonstrative sense of the 'Sturm und Drang' years, when individualism had been pursued for its own sake. Goethe himself said that in old age a man naturally turned towards what he called mysticism:

> Jedem Alter des Menschen antwortet eine gewisse Philosophie. Das Kind erscheint als Realist; denn es findet sich so überzeugt von dem Dasein der Birnen und Äpfel als von dem seinigen. Der Jüngling, von innern Leidenschaften bestürmt, muss auf sich selbst merken, sich vorfühlen: er wird zum Idealisten umgewandelt. Dagegen ein Skeptiker zu werden hat der Mann alle Ursache; er tut wohl zu zweifeln, ob das Mittel, das er zum Zwecke gewählt hat, auch das rechte sei. Vor dem Handeln, im Handeln hat er alle Ursache, den Verstand beweglich zu erhalten, damit er nicht nachher sich über eine falsche Wahl zu betrüben habe. Der Greis jedoch wird sich immer zum Mystizismus bekennen. Er sieht, dass so vieles vom Zufall abzuhängen scheint: das Unvernünftige gelingt, das Vernünftige schlägt fehl, Glück und Unglück stellen sich unerwartet ins gleiche; so ist es, so war es, und das hohe Alter beruhigt sich in dem, der da ist, der da war und der da sein wird.

To each age of man a certain philosophy answers. The child shows itself a realist; for it is convinced of the reality of pears and apples just as it is of its own. The youth, attacked from within by passions, has to be aware of himself, anticipate his own feelings: he is changed into an idealist. The grown man, on the other hand, has every reason to become a sceptic; he does well to doubt whether the means he has chosen to achieve his end are the right ones. Before acting, while acting he has every cause to keep his wits nimble, so that he will not have occasion later to regret a wrong choice. But the old man will always declare himself for the mystical philosophy. He sees that so much is apparently dependent on chance: unreasonable plans succeed, reasonable ones fail, fortune and misfortune unexpectedly cancel each other out; so it is, so it always has been, and high old age finds comfort in Him who is, who always has been and who always will be. (*Maximen und Reflexionen*)

As the world which Goethe had known and believed in seemed to crumble, he too became in his own eyes 'historical'. Accordingly he began to give a historical account of himself, seen at a distance, in his autobiography, the first volume of which appeared in 1811. Its title, *Dichtung und Wahrheit* (*Poetry and Truth*) indicates the keynote of all the autobiographical writings: they are all edited or imagined recollections of the truth rather than a factual record. Goethe defined his procedure in a letter of 12 January 1830 to the King of Bavaria.

> ... es war mein ernstestes Bestreben das eigentliche Grundwahre, das, insofern ich es einsah, in meinem Leben obgewaltet hatte, möglichst darzustellen und auszudrücken. Wenn aber ein solches in späteren Jahren nicht möglich ist, ohne die Rückerinnerung und also die Einbildungskraft wirken zu lassen, und man also immer in den Fall kommt gewissermassen das dichterische Vermögen auszuüben, so ist es klar, dass man mehr die Resultate und, wie wir uns das Vergangene jetzt denken, als die Einzelnheiten, wie sie sich damals ereigneten, aufstellen und hervorheben werde ... Dieses alles, was dem Erzählenden und der Erzählung angehört, habe ich hier unter dem Worte: Dichtung, begriffen, um mich des Wahren,

dessen ich mir bewusst war, zu meinem Zweck bedienen
zu können.

> ... it was my most earnest endeavour to represent and express, as
> best I could, the actual, true basic elements which had, as far as I
> could see, held sway in my life. But if such a task is not possible in
> later years without making use of one's retrospective memory and
> so of one's imagination, so that one always finds oneself using the
> poetic faculty to some extent, then it is clear that one will allow the
> results to dominate, and things past as we imagine them today, rather
> than the details of what actually happened. . . . All this, which is the
> part of the story-teller and of the telling, I have included here under
> the name of poetry, so that I could use for my purpose the truth of
> which I was aware.

The boundary between autobiography and fiction is always
indistinct. *Dichtung und Wahrheit* is not only a major autobiographical work, it also plays almost as important a part in
the development of the German 'Bildungsroman' as do the
Wilhelm Meister novels themselves. The other autobiographical
works, the *Italienische Reise* (*Italian Journey*), the first volume
of which appeared in 1816, and *Campagne in Frankreich*
(*Campaign in France*, 1820–2) are probably more reliable from
a purely factual standpoint, but that is not their major purpose
either, and they make considerable use of imaginative stylization.

2. Public affairs

Goethe saw Revolutionary, then Imperial France first apparently triumph, then fall. He realized that a new age in world
history was beginning. He saw the dangers to culture, civili-
zation and humanity inherent in many of the characteristic
features of emergent capitalist society: paper money (*Faust II*),
industrial mechanization and the division of labour (*Wilhelm
Meisters Wanderjahre*). The *Lehrjahre* already contains reference to America, but it does not appear intrinsically significant.
Lothario, we learn (Book IV, ch. 16; Book VII, ch. 3) had fought
there for the United States against England, but Lothario is a

soldier and one has the impression that he went there merely for the fighting, like the characters in Klinger's *Sturm und Drang*. But in the *Wanderjahre* America is the Utopian scene of a possible new start. This idea is also presented by Goethe in a short poem in the characteristically cryptic manner of his later years:

> Amerika, du hast es besser
> Als unser Kontinent, das alte,
> Hast keine verfallene Schlösser
> Und keine Basalte.
>
> Dich stört nicht im Innern
> Zu lebendiger Zeit
> Unnützes Erinnern
> Und vergeblicher Streit.

> America, you are better off than our old continent: you have no ruined castles and no basalts. You are not inwardly disturbed, in this living time, by useless memories and vain strife. (*Den vereinigten Staaten* [*To the United States*], ll. 1–8)

That is, America has no 'romantic' ruins and no volcanic rocks (in this Goethe was, of course, wrong), no misleading examples of disorder and violence in either its human or its geological history, so that a new form of organic society can peacefully evolve there. (Cf. below, p. 105.)

3. Science

Goethe continued for many years his researches into optics; and the basic intuition which informs his theory of colours is glimpsed in much of his late work. *Faust* is based on the polarity of light and darkness, God and the devil; in between is man, who is opaque or 'trüb'. 'Das Trübe', in Goethe's colour-theory, is a mystical rather than a genuinely scientific concept, denoting the imperfect conditions of earthly life. It is in these imperfect conditions that colours arise: the rainbow that Faust sees in the first scene of Part II. The rainbow was a stumbling-block to Goethe's scientific investigations, as it seems very plainly to demonstrate the Newtonian diffraction of light: not in an abstruse and artificial laboratory experiment, but as a real phenomenon of nature. But however difficult this may have been, its symbolic significance was clear.

Allein wie herrlich, diesem Sturm erspriessend,
Wölbt sich des bunten Bogens Wechseldauer,
Bald rein gezeichnet, bald in Luft zerfliessend,
Umher verbreitend duftig kühle Schauer.
Der spiegelt ab das menschliche Bestreben.
Ihm sinne nach, und du begreifst genauer;
Am farbigen Abglanz haben wir das Leben.

But how glorious, springing from this storm [a waterfall], arches the coloured rainbow in lasting change, now sharply drawn, now dissolving into air, spreading cool vaporous showers. *That* is the image of human aspirations. Think on it, and you will understand more fully: the coloured reflexion is what gives us our life. (*Faust*, ll. 4721–7)

But by entering into the spirit of metamorphosis, of permanence and change, which underlies the whole creation, one might find a way to transcend the limitations of 'das Trübe'.

Und so lang du das nicht hast,
Dieses: Stirb und werde!
Bist du nur ein trüber Gast
Auf der dunklen Erde.

And as long as you do not realize it, this: Die and become! you are only a dull guest on the dark earth. (*West-östlicher Divan: Selige Sehnsucht* [*Sacred Longing*], ll. 17–20)

Here 'trüb' seems to have something approaching the ordinary metaphorical meaning of 'dull'; but for Goethe this metaphor, like all the other metaphors of light and colour in his later writings, is derived from the whole complex of ideas which the *Farbenlehre* represents.

4. *Romanticism*

The first phase of the German Romantic movement got under way about 1799. The Romantics were opposed to the tenets of Weimar classicism as expounded by Goethe and Schiller, and disapproved of Schiller's work. They revered Goethe, however, especially for *Wilhelm Meisters Lehrjahre* which is the prototype of the Romantic 'Künstlerroman', or novel portraying the development of an artist. This development rests upon a misinterpretation of *Wilhelm Meister*—as was realized by Novalis when he re-read the novel and noticed what he had somehow failed to see before, that Wilhelm is not an artistic genius and gives up art to return to ordinary life. This to Novalis was 'artistic atheism'. Goethe was not a Romantic, though the Romantics found much to imitate in his works—Novalis' *Heinrich von Ofterdingen*, his 'anti-Meister', culminates in a 'Märchen' or fairy-tale told by the hero's mentor Klingsohr, and Klingsohr is perhaps Goethe and his 'Märchen' strongly suggests that in Goethe's *Unterhaltungen deutscher Ausgewanderten* (cf. above, p. 69 f.). In some of his later works Goethe repays the debt, notably in *Die Wahlverwandtschaften*, which treats of Romantic natural phenomena: mysterious sympathies and sensitivities, trances and divining. These recall the Romantics' scientific theories: it was in these, anti-mechanistic as his own, that Goethe could most easily sympathize with the Romantics. The use of Catholic imagery in *Die Wahlverwandtschaften* is also a Romantic feature. But *Die Wahlverwandtschaften* is not a Romantic work by a long way. And Goethe's irony is quite unlike the 'Romantic irony', token of the absolute and arbitrary power of the individual creative artist, propounded by Friedrich Schlegel. Nor did Goethe really approve of Romantic medievalism or nationalism, although (consistently with his earlier enthusiasm for Gothic architecture: cf. above, p. 15) he supported the scheme for completing Cologne Cathedral, in which these elements of Romanticism found their most tangible expression.[1] It is true that he had grown away from his Classicism, the style which he had regarded in the early '90s as of absolute, sole and abiding validity. But after Schiller's death he became a law unto himself, and cannot be considered to 'belong' to any literary movement.

5. Style

The style of Goethe's middle age and old age—already evolving in the classical period—is characterized by its symbolism, its pictorial quality, its irony and what one can best call stylization or formalization.

(a) *Symbolism.* Goethe defined symbolism as follows:

> Das ist die wahre Symbolik, wo das Besondere das Allgemeinere repräsentiert, nicht als Traum und Schatten, sondern als lebendig-augenblickliche Offenbarung des Unerforschlichen.

> There we find true symbolism, where the particular represents the more general, not as a dream and a shadow, but as instantaneous living revelation of the unfathomable. (*Maximen und Reflexionen*)

That is, Goethe's symbols are not *allegories* (or rarely so), whose precise meaning can be extracted from them. The casket in *Wilhelm Meisters Wanderjahre* is a good example. It is a mystery which is never explained: the reader may well want to know what is in it, or at least what happens when it is opened, but in this he is disappointed. The casket serves its function as a symbol merely by accompanying certain events and certain characters, thereby establishing a connexion—itself mysterious —between them.

[1] For an account of this, see W. D. Robson-Scott, *The Literary Background of the Gothic Revival in Germany*, Oxford 1965.

(b) *Pictorial quality.* We have observed that in *Hermann und Dorothea* and in *Wilhelm Meisters Lehrjahre* the action is frequently concentrated in stylized tableaux. The same is true in a high degree of *Faust II.* In the novel *Die Wahlverwandtschaften* scenes of great importance are concerned with actual presentation of *tableaux vivants* by the characters, the heroine Ottilie finally coming to represent the Virgin Mary. This pictorial manner of narration is obviously suited to symbolism. (Once again, the symbols are not allegories: Ottilie is in a sense a virgin mother, but one must beware of taking her 'beatification' too literally.) Some of the late lyric poetry also has an intense visual quality, notably some of the *Chinesisch-deutsche Tages- und Jahreszeiten* (cf. below, p. 96 f.), while the cycle *Wilhelm Tischbeins Idyllen* aims to recreate the effect of paintings by the well-known artist and near-contemporary of Goethe's (1751–1829).

(c) *Irony.* Irony is a means of distancing and objectivization. Its effect is frequently humorous or playful. It is by no means necessarily negative or derogatory in intent: indeed it may be quite the reverse, as is the application of the Homeric style in *Hermann und Dorothea.* Much of Goethe's late poetry treats the most serious themes, such as the ultimate philosophical problem of the One and the Many, with an extremely playful touch, a 'divine levity' as Ronald Peacock has called it.

> Freuet euch des wahren Scheins,
> Euch des ernsten Spieles:
> Kein Lebendiges ist ein Eins,
> Immer ist's ein Vieles.

> Take delight in this true illusion, this serious game: no living creature is a One, it is always a Many. (*Epirrhema*, ll. 7–10)

It is irony which enables Goethe in the extraordinary poem *Paria* to combine extremes of the sublime and the grotesque.

The 'ironic German' (Erich Heller's phrase) of our own century, Thomas Mann, attempts the same task, with the same or very similar subject-matter, in his story *Die vertauschten Köpfe* (*The Exchanged Heads*), though whether with Goethe's success the reader may judge for himself. It is also irony which enables Goethe to write amusingly but deeply seriously of marital and extra-marital sexual experience in the (usually suppressed) poem *Das Tagebuch* (*The Diary*), which he himself characterized as 'erotisch-moralisch'. And in the very last letter he wrote, addressed to Wilhelm von Humboldt on 17 March 1832, five days before he died, Goethe referred to *Faust II*, which he had completed, but decided not to publish in his lifetime, as 'diese sehr ernsten Scherze' ('these very serious jests').

(*d*) *Formalization*. This is related to irony, as a means of objectivization. It is also manifest already in the standardized epic phraseology of *Hermann und Dorothea*. It is manifest in the frequent use by Goethe in his later works of certain favourite adjectives, which like the 'herrlich' of *Hermann und Dorothea* can be described as generalized epithets of praise: 'heiter' (serene, cheerful), 'freundlich' (amiable), 'tüchtig' (doughty, sturdy), 'bedeutend' (meaningful, significant). Sometimes Goethe seems to retreat behind these words as into a kind of private language, in a way which can seem rather baffling or even off-putting to the reader, as when we read in the *Wanderjahre*

> Wir haben in diesem zweiten Buche die Verhältnisse unsrer alten Freunde *bedeutend steigern* sehen . . .
>
> We have now seen our old friends' relationships significantly intensified (*Wanderjahre*, Book II, 'Zwischenrede' after ch. 7; my italics)

Formalization also provides much of the highly stylized and compressed syntax of the later poetry, which we shall consider in the next section.

D

B. Lyric poetry

1. 'Gedankenlyrik'

Much of the late poetry is poetry of philosophical content, notably the poems grouped by Goethe under the rubric *Gott und Welt*. Some of this is 'ernstes Spiel', like *Epirrhema* quoted above, or its companion piece *Antepirrhema* which is an adaptation of some lines spoken by—of all people—Mephistopheles in *Faust*:

> So schauet mit bescheidnem Blick
> Der ewigen Weberin Meisterstück,
> Wie Ein Tritt tausend Fäden regt,
> Die Schifflein hinüber, herüber schiessen,
> Die Fäden sich begegnend fliessen,
> Ein Schlag tausend Verbindungen schlägt,
> Das hat sie nicht zusammengebettelt,
> Sie hat's von Ewigkeit angezettelt;
> Damit der ewige Meistermann
> Getrost den Einschlag werfen kann.

See then with modest glance the masterpiece of the eternal weaver-woman, see how one stroke on the pedal moves a thousand threads, the shuttles fly across this way and that, the threads run to meet each other, one movement produces a thousand connexions. This is no improvised contrivance, she has had her warp set up from all eternity, so that the eternal Master can happily weave away. (*Antepirrhema*; cf. *Faust*, ll. 1923–7)

The element of play is rarely completely absent, even in such a serious poem as *Urworte. Orphisch* (*Ancient Words of Wisdom, Orphic*), which lists the forces governing our lives as 'Dämon', or personal destiny; chance; love; necessity and hope. (The 'Dämon' of this poem may be compared with the characterization of 'das Dämonische' in *Dichtung und Wahrheit*, referred to on p. 27 above.) The poem *Vermächtnis* (*Testament*) appropriately sums up most of the major ideas of Goethe's philosophy (if that is not too precise a term).

The Indian legend *Paria*, although classified by Goethe as a ballad, might very well have been placed under the heading *Gott und Welt*, for the relationship between gods and man is precisely its theme. And much wisdom is summed up in gnomic 'Sprüche' or epigrammatic poems (now no longer in the metre of the classical epigram), the verse counterpart of the prose 'Maximen und Reflexionen'.

Willst du dich am Ganzen erquicken,
So musst du das Ganze in Kleinsten erblicken.

If you wish to draw nourishment from the whole, then you must recognize the whole in its smallest part.

Halte dich nur im stillen rein
Und lass es um dich wettern;
Je mehr du fühlst ein Mensch zu sein,
Desto ähnlicher bist du den Göttern.

Just calmly keep yourself pure and let the storms rage about you; the more you feel that you are a human being, the more like the gods you will be.

2. Love poetry

Of what we might call the 'pure lyric' poetry of Goethe's later years (not that this is without 'philosophical' overtones, nor that the 'philosophical' poetry is quite without 'lyric' qualities) some of the finest is love poetry. The three main groups are the sonnet-sequence of 1807–8; the love-poetry of the *West-östlicher Divan* (1814–18), celebrating the love of Goethe and Marianne von Willemer, and the poems relating to Goethe's last desperately passionate love-affair, that with Ulrike von Levetzow, which is commemorated above all in the *Trilogie der Leidenschaft* (*Trilogy of Passion*) centring on the so-called 'Marienbad Elegy' (1823). (Cf. Biography, p. 5 f. above.)

The range of style is enormous. The sonnets are still classical (and are so grouped in the chronological division of the *HA*), the discipline of the sonnet form itself aiding objectivity. Thus in the seventh sonnet, *Abschied* (*Parting*), Goethe can write:

> War unersättlich nach viel tausend Küssen,
> Und musst' mit Einem Kuss am Ende scheiden.
> Nach herber Trennung tiefempfundnem Leiden
> War mir das Ufer, dem ich mich entrissen,
>
> Mit Wohnungen, mit Bergen, Hügeln, Flüssen,
> Solang ich's deutlich sah, ein Schatz der Freuden;
> Zuletzt im Blauen blieb ein Augenweiden
> An fernentwichnen lichten Finsternissen.
>
> Und endlich, als das Meer den Blick umgrenzte,
> Fiel mir zurück ins Herz mein heiss Verlangen;
> Ich suchte mein Verlornes gar verdrossen.
>
> Da war es gleich, als ob der Himmel glänzte;
> Mir schien, als wäre nichts mir, nichts entgangen,
> Als hätt' ich alles, was ich je genossen.

I was insatiable after [?or: for] many thousand kisses, and had at the last to part with one kiss. After the deeply-felt sorrow of bitter parting, the shore from which I had torn myself was, with its dwelling-places, mountains, hills, and rivers, as long as I could still see it clearly, a treasure-house of joys; finally my eyes feasted on the delicate shadows of the far-off blue horizon [these two lines are impossible to translate literally]. And last of all as the sea stretched as far as I could see on all sides, my hot yearning fell back into my heart; dejected I searched for what I had lost. Then it was as if the heavens shone; it seemed to me that nothing, nothing had escaped me, as if I still possessed everything that I had ever enjoyed.

What this poem stylizes and distances, the *Elegie* presents more passionately and painfully.

> Der Kuss, der letzte, grausam süss, zerschneidend
> Ein herrliches Geflecht verschlungner Minnen,

Nun eilt, nun stockt der Fuss, die Schwelle meidend,
Als trieb' ein Cherub flammend ihn von hinnen;
Das Auge starrt auf düstrem Pfad verdrossen,
Es blickt zurück, die Pforte steht verschlossen.

The kiss, the last, cruelly sweet, cutting asunder a glorious fabric of
interwoven love. Now the foot hurries, now it hesitates, shunning
the threshold as if an angel drove it away with flame; the eye, on its
gloomy path, stares dejected, it looks back, the door stands barred.
(ll. 19–24)

The *Buch Suleika* in the *West-östlicher Divan* celebrates the
harmony of love. Some of the poems in this book are actually
by Marianne von Willemer, though Goethe has altered them
slightly.

3. Eastern styles

The East provided three sources of colouring for Goethe's
later poetry. The *West-östlicher Divan* is an imitation, or
perhaps rather an emulation, of Persian poetry and in particular
the *Divan* of Mohammed Shams-ed-din Hafiz, the great
Persian poet of the fourteenth century. The word 'divan'
means 'assembly' or 'collection'. But, as the adjective 'west-
östlich' implies, Goethe does not attempt a consistent formal
imitation of Eastern poetry, as did such poets as Rückert and
Platen a few years later. This is Western poetry but with an
Eastern flavouring, sometimes used for mystification, with
deliberately recondite allusions:

Wisset ihr, wie *Schehâb-eddin*
Sich auf *Arafat* entmantelt;
Niemand haltet ihr für törig,
Der in seinem Sinne handelt.

You know how Shehab-ed-din took off his cloak on Arafat; you will
not think anyone foolish who acts in the same spirit. (*Geheimstes*,
ll. 13–16)

—sometimes as a playfully transparent disguise, as in these lines addressed by 'Hatem' to 'Suleika', where the missing rhyme-word is obviously the poet's real name:

> Du beschämst wie Morgenröte
> Jener Gipfel ernste Wand,
> Und noch einmal fühlet Hatem
> Frühlingshauch und Sommerbrand.

You shame like the dawn those peaks' severe wall, and once more Hatem feels the breath of spring and the burning heat of summer. ('Locken, haltet mich . . .', ll. 9–12)

Sometimes East and West are humorously juxtaposed:

> *Schenke*
> Welch ein Zustand! Herr, so späte
> Schleichst du heut aus deiner Kammer;
> Perser nennen's Bidamag buden,
> Deutsche sagen Katzenjammer.

CUPBEARER: What a state! Master, so late you creep out of your room today; the Persians call it 'bidamag buden', the Germans say 'cats-grief' [i.e. a hangover]. ('Welch ein Zustand . . .', ll. 1–4)

India provides the setting for the ballad *Der Gott und die Bajadere* and for the *Paria* trilogy. Here the form is entirely Goethe's own, the East merely providing suitably exotic local colour for poems whose content is highly paradoxical.

Finally, Goethe turned to China for a poetic style. In 1829 he produced a cycle of fourteen short poems entitled *Chinesisch-deutsche Jahres- und Tageszeiten* (*Chinese-German Seasons and Hours*). Again, these do not imitate specific forms of Chinese poetry, but in their pictorial quality and their stylized concentration and simplification they are intended to evoke the character of Chinese poetry and Chinese landscape painting.

One in particular of this cycle, 'Dämmrung senket sich . . .',
(No. 8), is generally recognized as one of the greatest of all
Goethe's lyrics. It evokes in the style of his old age the nocturnal
landscape familiar, with its symbolic significance, from poems
of many years before (cf. above, p. 42):

Dämmrung senkte sich von oben,
Schon ist alle Nähe fern;
Doch zuerst emporgehoben
Holden Lichts der Abendstern!
Alles schwankt ins Ungewisse,
Nebel schleichen in die Höh';
Schwarzvertiefte Finsternisse
Widerspiegelnd ruht der See.

Nun am östlichen Bereiche
Ahn' ich Mondenglanz und -glut,
Schlanker Weiden Haargezweige
Scherzen auf der nächsten Flut.
Durch bewegter Schatten Spiele
Zittert Lunas Zauberschein,
Und durchs Auge schleicht die Kühle
Sänftigend ins Herz hinein.

Dusk sank down from above, already all nearness is distant; but
first uplifted with its sweet light the evening star! Every outline becomes indistinct, mists creep upwards; the lake reposes, reflecting
black-deepened darknesses. Now in the eastern region I detect the
brightness and glow of the moon; slender willows' hair-like twigs
jest upon the nearby water. Through the play of moving shadows
quivers Luna's magic shining, and through the eye the coolness
creeps assuaging into the heart.

Once again, Goethe does not aim at consistent 'Oriental'
colouring, but can quite happily in this context refer to the moon
by her Latin name, *Luna*.

4. Poetic language

Klopstock had introduced into German poetry a number of unfamiliar devices of syntax and word-formation, often imitated from Latin or Greek, with a view to creating a distinctly 'poetic' language, contrary to the ideal of such critics as Gottsched who had taught that poetry should obey the same logic as prose. Goethe in his 'Sturm und Drang' period had used such devices for their expressive power. In his classical poetry they are used for their antique flavour (cf. above, p. 64). In the late poetry these and similar devices are used for the purpose of concentration. Meaning is so finely distilled that it seems to come across with unique immediacy, but the reader should nevertheless pause and consider the methods by which this is achieved: methods of extraordinary artistry. In 'Dämmrung senkte sich . . .' almost every line is grammatically remarkable—not *un*grammatically remarkable like *Mailied* or *An Schwager Kronos*—and many favourite devices of Goethe's are found here: suppression of articles, adverbial genitives ('holden Lichts'), past and present participial constructions—only when we get to 'widerspiegelnd' do we discover that the preceding phrase is its object—and new compound coinages ('schwarzvertieft', 'Haargezweige'). A construction of particularly frequent occurrence is the combination of a noun—often itself a compound—with a preceding phrase in the genitive: 'schlanker Weiden Haargezweige', 'bewegter Schatten Spiele'. One could perhaps coin a grammatical term for this and call it a genitive of concentration. It might be compared with that favourite Shakespearian construction 'the (noun) and (noun) of (noun)' (discussed by William Empson in Chapter II of *Seven Types of Ambiguity*), which in a similar way creates a close syntactical concentration of a large amount of meaning and association.

The Indian legend *Paria*, which Eckermann records Goethe's likening to 'eine aus Stahldrähten geschmiedete Damaszenerklinge' ('a damascene blade forged from steel wires'), presents numerous examples of this extraordinary manipulation of

language. In the following lines from *Legende*, the central
poem of the *Paria* trilogy, I have indicated them by italics:

Wasser holen geht die reine
Schöne Frau des hohen Brahmen,
Des verehrten, fehlerlosen,
Ernstester Gerechtigkeit . . .

To fetch water goes the pure beautiful wife of the high Brahmin, of
the revered, the faultless one, *of* gravest justice. (ll. 1–4)

Heute kommt *die morgendliche*
Im Gebet zu Ganges' Fluten . . .

Today comes she-in-the-morning to Ganges' waters. (ll. 15–16)

Plötzlich *überraschend spiegelt*
Aus *des höchsten Himmels Breiten*
Über ihr vorübereilend
Allerliebliche Gestalt
Hehren Jünglings, den *des Gottes*
Uranfänglich-schönes Denken
Aus dem ew'gen Busen schuf;
Solchen schauend fühlt ergriffen
Von verwirrenden Gefühlen
Sie das innere tiefste Leben . . .

Suddenly surprising [her] reflects [one would expect 'spiegelt *sich*',
or something like 'sie sieht gespiegelt', 'she sees reflected'] from the
highest heaven's breadths hastening by above her [the] loveliest
figure of [a] noble youth, whom the god's primordial-beautiful
thought created from the eternal bosom; beholding such she [the
subject is in a very odd place] feels seized by confusing feelings the
innermost depth of [her] life. (ll. 18–27)

Sie erblickt nur *hohler Wirbel*
Grause Tiefen unter sich . . .

She only sees hollow whirlpools' grim depths beneath her. (ll. 35–6:
the preceding genitive without article is a much more unusual construction in German than in English.)

C. The novel

In 1807 Goethe began to write a series of 'Novellen' or short stories centring on the theme of 'Entsagung', resignation or renunciation. These began to form themselves into a novel, the sequel to *Wilhelm Meisters Lehrjahre*, presenting the theme of 'Bildung' less under its individual than under its social aspects. One of the stories originally intended for the *Wanderjahre*, *Die Wahlverwandtschaften* (*Elective Affinities*) took such powerful hold on Goethe's imagination that it grew into a separate novel, and as such appeared in 1808. The first version of the *Wanderjahre* appeared in 1821, with the designation 'Erster Teil' ('Part I'); but for the second edition of 1829 the work was submitted to a thoroughgoing revision.

1. 'Entsagung'

The full title of the second Wilhelm Meister novel is *Wilhelm Meisters Wanderjahre oder die Entsagenden* (*Wilhelm Meister's Years of Travel, or The Renunciants*). This indicates the real theme of the novel—and the theme which, as its genesis shows, is at least the starting-point of *Die Wahlverwandtschaften* too. 'Renunciation' is the subordination of one goal or goals in life—happiness, love, the fulfilment of some immediate purpose—to another or others which are recognized to be higher. It is in its most general sense a moral ordering of life based upon a recognition of the limitations of the human condition. Faced with a situation in which love and the desire for happiness conflict with the demands of society and morality, the characters in *Die Wahlverwandtschaften* vary in their capacity for renunciation. For Charlotte and the Captain, it is easy; perhaps too easy. Thus Charlotte finds satisfaction, even pleasure, in her ability to set her marital duties above her love for the Captain:

> Gerührt kniete sie nieder, sie wiederholte den Schwur, den sie Eduarden vor dem Altar getan. Freundschaft, Neigung,

Entsagen gingen vor ihr in heitern Bildern vorüber. Sie
fühlte sich innerlich wiederhergestellt. Bald ergreift sie
eine süsse Müdigkeit und ruhig schläft sie ein.

Moved, she knelt down, she repeated the vow which she had made
to Eduard before the altar. Friendship, inclination, renunciation
followed one another in serene images before her. She felt inwardly
restored. Soon a sweet drowsiness overcomes here and peacefully she
falls asleep. (*Die Wahlverwandtschaften*, Part I, ch. 12)

On the other hand Eduard is quite incapable of renunciation;
and Ottilie, the heroine, goes through a great struggle in her
devotion to him. After his departure we are firmly told that

Ottilie hatte Eduarden nicht entsagt.

Ottilie had not renounced Eduard. (Part I, ch. 17)

After the birth of Charlotte's child Ottilie believes that she can
renounce Eduard while yet continuing to love him:

Sie wünschte nur das Wohl ihres Freundes, sie glaubte
sich fähig, ihm zu entsagen, sogar ihn niemals wieder-
zusehen, wenn sie ihn nur glücklich wisse.

She desired only the wellbeing of her friend, she thought herself
capable of renouncing him, even of never seeing him again, if only
she knew that he was happy. (Part II, ch. 9)

But after the catastrophe, for which Ottilie bears the most
immediate responsibility, she renounces completely—at least,
consciously she does so:

... sie hatte sich in der Tiefe ihres Herzens nur unter der
Bedingung des völligen Entsagens verziehen, und diese
Bedingung war für alle Zukunft unerlässlich.

> . . . in the depths of her heart she had forgiven herself only on con-
> dition of total renunciation, and this condition was binding for all
> time. (Part II, ch. 15)

But even this is by no means the end of the story.

Die Wahlverwandtschaften teaches no clear-cut moral lesson;
indeed many of its first readers thought it a highly immoral
book. And Goethe's pronouncement to Eckermann on 6 May
1827 has seemed to many almost the reverse of the truth,
perhaps even a deliberate obfuscation of it:

> Das einzige Produkt von *grösserem* Umfang, wo ich mir
> bewusst bin, nach Darstellung einer durchgreifenden Idee
> gearbeitet zu haben, wären etwa meine „Wahlverwandt-
> schaften". Der Roman ist dadurch für den Verstand fass-
> lich geworden . . .

> The only larger-scale work of mine in which I am aware of having
> aimed at representing a single idea running throughout it would be,
> I suppose, my *Elective Affinities*. The novel did as a result become
> accessible to the understanding . . .

Benno von Wiese describes it as 'das undurchdringlichste und
vielleicht vieldeutigste Buch, das Goethe geschrieben hat'—
'the most impenetrable and perhaps richest in meanings of all
the books Goethe wrote' (*HA* 6, 653). It is not at all clear from
Die Wahlverwandtschaften that love ought to be surrendered to
morality—H. G. Barnes's interpretation of the novel characterizes Ottilie as a saint of love. And one thing which the novel
does strongly suggest—yet which the *Wanderjahre*, which of
all Goethe's works most resolutely excludes tragedy, admits
hardly if at all—is that it is not always possible for man to
make the moral ordering of his life typified in the notion of
'Entsagung'. He may well be for at least part of the time under
the control of superior natural forces.

2. Nature

The relation of man to the⁻forces of nature is an important theme of *Die Wahlverwandtschaften*, and nature is an important source of motifs and symbols: landscape, water, flowers. The characters devote a great deal of time and energy to landscape gardening—that is, to controlling and manipulating nature outside themselves as well as (or instead of) within. Eduard, and even more so Ottilie, seem to exist in sympathy and close communication with nature, as is indicated by such things as their sympathetic headaches and Ottilie's success in the divining experiments. And of course, the 'Wahlverwandtschaften' or 'elective affinities' ('attractiones electivae') of the title is a term taken from contemporary natural science. The new title, *Kindred by Choice*, given by H. M. Waidson to his recent translation of the novel obscures this fact, which is of some importance. In the fourth chapter of the novel the chemical notion of 'Wahlverwandtschaft', the force which brings about a reaction of the type $AB + CD = AD + BC$, is explained. Charlotte asks whether it is right to use such an anthropomorphic term to describe the actions and reactions of chemical elements. The novel as a whole implies the question whether human actions and reactions are, like those of which chemistry treats, purely mechanical, or whether the agents involved do have a genuine power of choice.

> „ . . . Hier ist eine Trennung, eine neue Zusammensetzung entstanden, und man glaubt sich nunmehr berechtigt, sogar das Wort Wahlverwandtschaft anzuwenden, weil es wirklich aussieht, als wenn ein Verhältnis dem andern vorgezogen, eins vor dem andern erwählt würde."
> „Verzeihen Sie mir," sagte Charlotte, „wie ich dem Naturforscher verzeihe; aber ich würde hier niemals eine Wahl, eher eine Naturnotwendigkeit erblicken, und diese kaum; denn es ist am Ende vielleicht gar nur die Sache der Gelegenheit. Gelegenheit macht Verhältnisse, wie sie

Diebe macht; und wenn von Ihren Naturkörpern die Rede
ist, so scheint mir die Wahl bloss in den Händen des
Chemikers zu liegen, der diese Wesen zusammenbringt.
Sind sie aber einmal beisammen, dann gnade ihnen Gott!"

. . . 'Here a separation, a new combination have occurred, and now it
is even felt justifiable to use the word elective affinity, because it
really does look as though one relationship were preferred to the
other, one elected rather than the other.'—'Forgive me,' said
Charlotte, 'as I forgive the scientist; but I should never have seen any
choice in this, rather a natural necessity, and scarcely even that; for it
is probably only a matter of opportunity after all. Opportunity makes
relationships, as it makes thieves [proverb]; and as far as your natural
elements are concerned, the only choice seems to me to lie in the
hands of the chemist who brings these things together. Once they are
together, though, then may God be merciful to them . . .' (Part I,
ch. 4)

3. Society
Die Wahlverwandtschaften is not primarily a social novel, but
the characters may to some extent be seen as typical representa-
tives of their class, the pre-revolutionary landed aristocracy and
its dependents. This is particularly true of such peripheral
characters as Luciane or the Count and Baroness. The action
is deliberately isolated from the major events of the world.
Eduard goes off to the wars (we do not even know what wars)
purely as a romantic gesture. But it is possible to interpret the
novel as in part a critique of a society whose forms and institu-
tions—typified by the institution of marriage—have so ossified
as to make meaningful human relationships impossible. The
Wanderjahre on the other hand is very much concerned with
social problems characteristic of the age of transition which
Goethe now recognized he was witnessing. These displace the
ideal of individual 'Bildung' which dominates the *Lehrjahre* (cf.
above, p. 71 ff.). Indeed the brusque Jarno, in his conversation
with Wilhelm in the opening chapters of the novel, casts doubt
upon the absolute validity of this ideal.

„Man hat aber doch eine vielseitige Bildung für vorteilhaft
und notwendig gehalten."—„Sie kann es auch sein zu ihrer
Zeit," versetzte jener; „Vielseitigkeit bereitet eigentlich
nur das Element vor, worin der Einseitige wirken kann,
dem eben jetzt genug Raum gegeben ist. Ja, es ist jetzo
die Zeit der Einseitigkeiten; wohl dem, der es begreift, für
sich und andre in diesem Sinne wirkt."

'But a many-sided education has been held to be advantageous and
necessary.' 'It can be when the times are appropriate,' replied the other
[Jarno]; 'many-sidedness in fact only prepares the medium for the
effective activity of the one-sided specialist, who at this very moment
has scope enough granted to him. Yes, this is the age of specialisms;
good fortune to him who can understand this and act for himself
and others on this basis.' (*Wanderjahre*, Book 1, ch. 4)

The novel considers such eminently practical socio-economic
problems as the consequences of overpopulation and industrialization. No definitive solution is proposed, but some of the
novel's characters aim at practical reform of European conditions, others at making a fresh start by emigrating to America
(cf. above, p. 86). At the same time the novel contains a great
deal that is much more remote, such as the Utopian 'Pedagogic
Province' and the strange figure of Makarie, whose name
means 'blessed' and who is said to exist in a kind of inexpressible
spiritual sympathy with the entire solar system.

4. Narrative technique

Die Wahlverwandtschaften and the *Wanderjahre* are very
different in form. The earlier work is tightly knit and is often
said to exhibit the characteristics of the 'Novelle' rather than
the novel: primacy of plot and action, subordination of
character, personages with purely functional names ('the
Count', 'the Captain', 'the Architect'). The *Wanderjahre* on
the other hand appears extremely diffuse in form. As in *Faust II*,
the titular protagonist recedes to the periphery and becomes,
for much of the work at any rate, a mere spectator. The final

shape of the novel also appears to be, despite the extensive revision to which it was subjected, vague and arbitrary. It does however share certain important technical features with *Die Wahlverwandtschaften*, features characteristic of the style of Goethe's later years.

(*a*) *Symbolism and 'mirroring'*. Both novels are held together by patterns of symbols, the setting forth of which takes precedence, particularly in the *Wanderjahre*, over exposition of character and situation and development of motivation in the conventional sense. The landscape symbolism in *Die Wahlverwandtschaften* has already been mentioned; drowning and the danger of drowning are recurrent motifs in both novels. The danger of too precise interpretation of symbols has also been pointed out. In *Die Wahlverwandtschaften* the character Eduard is himself an over-zealous interpreter of symbols, who confers on signs and coincidences a significance which they do not necessarily possess: by believing in fate he himself becomes its instrument.

Both novels also employ a technique of mirroring their themes from different angles by means of interpolated subsidiary narrations. The *Wanderjahre* includes half-a-dozen 'Novellen', related in various ways to the main action, some of them running into it—the characters in the 'Novelle' subsequently appearing in the 'Rahmengeschichte' or main 'framework' narrative. Originally intended as one of these interpolations, *Die Wahlverwandtschaften* in its final form itself contains a similar interpolated 'Novelle' (Part II, ch. 10), mirroring the main action. This mirroring technique is on a large scale what the repetition of symbols is on a smaller one, serving to impress certain themes and motifs on our minds as we read. *Die Wahlverwandtschaften* also incorporates extracts from Ottilie's diary or commonplace book, which provide generalized statements which can again be related to the particular statement made by the main action; the maxims and observations in the *Wanderjahre* fulfil the same function.

(*b*) *Narrative irony*. Modern theory and criticism of fiction attaches considerable importance to the question of 'point of view' or the identity of the narrative voice. The narrator of a novel may be identifiable with the author, so that we are told authoritatively how the story and the characters are to be interpreted. The narrator may be a distinct character *within* the novel itself—Ellen in *Wuthering Heights*, Marlow in several of Conrad's stories and novels, Zeitblom in Thomas Mann's *Doktor Faustus*. Or there may be an unidentified fictive narrator occupying some position between these two extremes. All Goethe's novels are of interest from this point of view, and the importance of the narrator in *Die Wahlverwandtschaften*, and of *his* (as distinct from Goethe's) interpretation of the events of the novel, has in particular been stressed by Paul Stöcklein (*Wege zum späten Goethe*) and in the full-length English study of the novel by H. G. Barnes (*Goethe's Die Wahlverwandtschaften*, Oxford 1967). The view advanced by these critics is important, but not uncontroversial. Clearly Goethe is using the ironic narrative voice to distance himself from the work in some way; but he may well be doing no more than reminding us that the characters and situations are fictional. In thus disclaiming responsibility for any of the opinions expressed in the novel, he is by no means evidently inviting us to work out what he 'really thinks': his aim is to touch our emotions. He may even be warning us *not* to try and 'interpret' too much, like the narrator of the 'Märchen' in the *Unterhaltungen* (cf. above, p. 69 f.). Similarly in the *Wanderjahre* the narrator makes ironic play with the reader's expectations and with the narrative situation, confusing framework and interpolations, as mentioned above, or interposing cryptic comments such as that quoted on p. 91.

D. Faust II

In 1797 Goethe decided that his Faust drama would have to be in two parts. During the final phase of writing Part I, he **was** also working already on Part II: on what eventually became the third act, a 'klassisch-romantische Phantasmagorie' in which Faust meets Helen of Troy (part of the traditional Faustian material). But the second part was to take almost as long to finish as the first. In 1816 Goethe made a summary of the proposed course of the action for *Dichtung und Wahrheit* in the belief that the work would never be completed. But Eckermann offered encouragement, and Goethe came to the end of what can truly be described as his life's work in 1831. He made a few small revisions shortly before his death.

1. Faust I and Faust II

The second part may in externals—the shift of scene from the restricted, small-town milieu of the Gretchen tragedy to the Emperor's court, and the involvement of the hero in public affairs, high finance and war—be seen as fulfilling Mephistopheles' promise:

> Wir sehn die kleine, dann die grosse Welt (cf. above, p. 82).

More sophisticatedly it can perhaps—it is a big perhaps, even if it is possible to elucidate the meaning of the terms with any precision—be seen as carrying out the scheme for the two parts, the so-called 'Paralipomenon No. 1', which Goethe made in 1797.

> Lebens-Genuss der Person von aussen gesehn 1. Teil. in der Dumpfheit Leidenschaft.
> Thaten-Genuss nach aussen 2. Teil. Und Genuss mit Bewusstsein. Schönheit.
> Schöpfungs-Genuss von innen. Epilog im Chaos auf dem Weg zur Hölle.

Personal enjoyment of life seen from without Part 1—instinctual—passion. Outward-directed enjoyment of action Part 2 and enjoyment with awareness. Beauty. Enjoyment of creation from within. Epilogue in Chaos on the way to Hell.

But the two Parts seem remote from each other: it is only in Act V that the thread of action is resumed, the terms of the pact (which itself apparently caused Goethe such difficulty in Part I) recalled, and Faust's destiny resolved. This has led some critics to maintain that the second part has no serious connexion with the first, but is an independent poem, and has nothing to do with the ostensible hero, Faust, at all. However, the work does conclude with the hero's salvation, so we may begin by assuming dramatic continuity between the Parts and consider the work from this point of view.

2. Faust's salvation

Faust's opening monologue immediately introduces the familiar leading theme of 'Streben' (cf. above, p. 79 f.):

> Des Lebens Pulse schlagen frisch lebendig,
> Ätherische Dämmerung milde zu begrüssen;
> Du, Erde, warst auch diese Nacht beständig
> Und atmest neu erquickt zu meinen Füssen,
> Beginnest schon, mit Lust mich zu umgeben,
> Du regst und rührst ein kräftiges Beschliessen,
> Zum höchsten Dasein immerfort zu streben.

The pulses of life beat with renewed vigour, sweetly to greet aethereal twilight; you, earth, were constant throughout this night too and breathe newly-refreshed at my feet, begin already to surround me with delight, you move and stir a powerful resolve always to strive to the highest form of existence. (ll. 4679–85)

Public affairs, art and learning (embodied in the pursuit of Helen of Troy through the ramifications of the antique mythological world in the 'Klassische Walpurgisnacht' and in the subsequent union of Faust and Helen), war and civil engineering are all spheres of human activity and aspiration which can serve as media to illustrate his striving. But there is general disagreement among critics as to whether Faust makes any spiritual or moral progress in or as a result of his striving; whether there is any difference of ethical quality between his land-reclamation scheme and his previous activities (e.g. whether it is altruistic or egoistic); what exactly happens to Faust, apart from his physical loss of sight, as a result of his encounter with 'Sorge' ('care')—and even about the identity and significance of one of Sorge's companions: is 'Schuld' to be equated with 'guilt' or with some more material force such as 'debt'? There is disagreement about whether Faust actually wins or loses the wager with Mephistopheles, which in Part I had been formulated thus:

> Werd' ich zum Augenblicke sagen:
> Verweile doch! du bist so schön!
> Dann magst du mich in Fesseln schlagen,
> Dann will ich gern zu Grunde gehn!

If ever I say to the passing moment: Stay! you are so fair! then you may clap me in irons, then I will gladly go to my ruin. (ll. 1699–1702)

The last words which Faust utters, imagining the fulfilment of his schemes, are:

> Zum Augenblicke dürft' ich sagen:
> Verweile doch, du bist so schön!
> Es kann die Spur von meinen Erdetagen
> Nicht in Äonen untergehn.—
> Im Vorgefühl von solchem hohen Glück
> Geniess' ich jetzt den höchsten Augenblick.

Then I might say to the passing moment: stay! you are so fair! The trace of my earthly days cannot disappear in aeons.—In anticipation of such high happiness I now enjoy the highest moment. (ll. 11581–6)

In the first of these lines Goethe had originally written 'darf', present indicative; he changed it to 'dürfte', conditional—

but left 'geniesse' in the present indicative. Has Faust stopped striving—or is he to be held to have kept on striving to the limit of his physical powers? Is this ceaseless striving, if such it be, held to justify Faust? In the *Wanderjahre* Goethe had said:

Unbedingte Tätigkeit, von welcher Art sie sei, macht zuletzt bankerott.

Unconditional (or 'absolute') activity, of whatever kind, leads ultimately to bankruptcy. (Also in *Maximen und Reflexionen*)

The novel had been devoted to the exposition of the theme of renunciation; Faust is the very type of the non-renunciant, the man who faced with the paralysing onslaught of 'Sorge' proclaims as his gospel of life:

Im Weiterschreiten find' er Qual und Glück,
Er, unbefriedigt jeden Augenblick!

In striding onward let man find pain and happiness, he never satisfied at any moment! (ll. 11451-2)

The outcome is uncertain: so much so that Goethe finds it necessary to resolve Faust's fate by intervention from above, which creates still further interpretative problems. Angels descend, distract Mephistopheles just as he is preparing to pounce on Faust's soul escaping from his body, and carry the immortal remnant off to heaven, proclaiming:

Gerettet ist das edle Glied
Der Geisterwelt vom Bösen,
Wer immer strebend sich bemüht,
Den können wir erlösen.
Und hat an ihm die Liebe gar
Von oben teilgenommen,
Begegnet ihm die selige Schar
Mit herzlichem Willkommen.

The noble limb of the spiritual world is saved from evil [? or 'from the Evil One']; *whoever struggles in ceaseless striving, him we can redeem.* [The emphasis is Goethe's.] And if love from above has touched him, the blessed hosts meet him with heartfelt welcome. (ll. 11934–41)

Eudo Mason distinguishes what he calls a 'Faustian' line of interpretation, according to which Faust is saved because of his striving; a 'Christian' line, according to which he is saved by divine grace, the intercession of Gretchen playing its part; and a 'Pelagian' line which supposes some interaction of the two forces and some actual moral improvement on Faust's part. All three are however, he concludes, unsatisfactory (*Goethe's Faust*, pp. 366 ff.). But whatever the justification of Faust's salvation, saved he certainly is; Mephistopheles the nihilist is defeated, and an affirmative verdict is passed upon life.

3. The 'digressions'

This conclusion does perhaps after all lend some support to the view that *Faust II* is not really about Faust at all, but about the whole of life: its ultimate statement being not that the soul of the individual called Faust is saved, but that life is good, that Mephistopheles is wrong to prefer 'das Ewig-Leere' ('eternal emptiness': l. 11603). The different spheres of activity referred to above (p. 109) are really presented *for their own sake*. The work thus becomes large enough for Goethe legitimately to introduce odd favourite topics of his own such as paper money (Act I) and the cosmological debate of his own day between the 'Neptunists' and the 'Vulcanists' represented in Act II by Thales and Anaxagoras respectively, about the origins of the universe. Goethe continued to believe in the organic unity-in-diversity of all life, including human society. He was unwilling to believe that violent, disruptive forces could, as the Vulcanists averred, have played any significant part in the evolution of an ordered cosmos; and he saw the introduction of paper money as a disruption of the 'natural' economic basis of society. At this point we recall the Marxist interpretation of *Faust* by Lukács, who reminds us that Goethe witnessed the birth of modern industrial capitalism and was well aware of, and much concerned by, the growth of this new force. Similar views to Goethe's were held by many of his contemporaries: in England, for example, by Burke and Cobbett.

Such apparent digressions from the central themes of the work are perfectly relevant to what is nothing less than a poetic representation of the entire Goethean cosmos. The persistence throughout *Faust II* of the figures of Faust and Mephistopheles, the reappearance of other characters from Part I such as Wagner and Gretchen, even the final evocation of the original pact, are on a reading such as this purely formal devices. They give the work the required minimum of external unity. But its true unity is provided by the universality of its themes and by the underlying patterns, groups and chains of symbols which have been identified and expounded most notably by Wilhelm Emrich in his study *Die Symbolik von Faust II*.

4. Structure and style

Whichever view we take of its overall unity and meaning, *Faust II* is (with the possible exception of the *Wanderjahre*) the most loosely-structured, the most episodic of all Goethe's works. The 'Mummenschanz' or masquerade in Act I is an image of the whole work: a succession of animated tableaux. *Faust II* is also the supreme example of Goethe's pictorial style. The masquerade, culminating in the appearance of Faust in the guise of Plutus, does in fact owe inspiration to Mantegna's *Triumph of Caesar* (which Goethe knew only from reproductions: the originals can be seen at Hampton Court); the end of Act II is a 'Triumph of Galatea', recalling, for example, Raphael's treatment of this theme; and the final pages of Act V with the soaring *Mater gloriosa* and her attendants suggest nothing so much as a typical South German baroque church interior. The third act is described in 1826 as a 'Phantasmagorie' and as a 'Zwischenspiel' or interlude, which suggests that it is not supposed to take place on the same plane of reality as the rest of the action—perhaps in a dream? Figures such as the 'Knabe Lenker' (boy charioteer) in Act I, Homunculus in Act II, Euphorion in Act III, even, it has been recently suggested,[1] the Emperor in Act IV, are parallels to Faust who reflect and to some extent take over his focal role, just as the 'Novellen' in the *Wanderjahre* mirror the main themes and action.

Even more than Part I, Part II of *Faust* exemplifies in its style the cosmic principle of unity-in-diversity. Prose has disappeared, but the metrical variations are even greater than those of Part I, and again Goethe moves easily from one metre and style to another, whether the transition be smooth or abrupt. Faust's opening monologue is in *terza rima*, a rich and solemn metre (five-stressed lines rhymed aba bcb cdc, etc.: cf. the lines quoted above, pp. 109 and 87). The 'Helen' act imitates the long rolling iambic lines of Greek tragedy:

> Bewundert viel und viel gescholten, Helena,
> Vom Strande komm' ich, wo wir erst gelandet sind . . .

Much admired and much reproved, I, Helen, come from the seashore where we have just landed (ll. 8488–9)

(These lines are confusingly called *trimeters* because they contain three 'dipodies' or *pairs* of feet, thus:

$$\cup \; \grave{-} \mid \cup \; \acute{-} \parallel \cup \; \grave{-} \mid \cup \; \acute{-} \parallel \cup \; \grave{-} \mid \cup \; \acute{-})$$

Even the formal French alexandrine, discredited since the defeat of Gottsched's version of classicism in the mid-eighteenth century, returns here in the final scene of Act IV, complete with

[1] By Paul Requadt in an article in the *Jahrbuch der deutschen Schillergesellschaft*, 1964.

regular alternation of masculine (monosyllabic) and feminine (dissyllabic) rhymes, as the appropriate metre for the feudal formalities of the Emperor's court:

> Es sei nun, wie ihm sei! uns ist die Schlacht gewonnen,
> Des Feinds zerstreute Flucht im flachen Feld zerronnen.
> Hier steht der leere Thron, verräterischer Schatz,
> Von Teppichen umhüllt, verengt umher der Platz.

Be that as it may! we have won the battle; the enemy, fleeing and scattered, has disappeared in the flat fields. Here stands the empty throne, treacherous treasure, veiled with draperies, narrow the space around it. (ll. 10849–52)

There are certainly plenty of 'sehr ernste Scherze', particularly in the first two acts, but also some exquisite lyricism—in fact some of the very finest of Goethe's late poetry. On the meaning of *Faust II*, on the question of its dramatic or thematic unity, on its merits as a whole, critical debate is unlikely ever to cease; but that it is a treasure-house of profound insights and illuminations, expressed with the greatest possible poetic virtuosity, can hardly be disputed.

6

Conclusion

Panoramic ability schreibt mir ein englischer Kritiker
zu, wofür ich allerschönstens zu danken habe.

'Panoramic ability' an English critic says I have—thank you very
kindly, I'm sure. (*Maximen und Reflexionen*)

So much for the English critic—or, indeed, any critic—who
attempts to sum up in a few words the life's work of Germany's
greatest poet. Even the writer of a modest introduction such
as the present work may feel, indeed, should feel himself open
to the charge of presumption. However, I hope that the reader
will have formed some not too inaccurate picture of the range
and variety, also of the constant preoccupations of Goethe's
work, and that this picture will provide a perspective in which
the individual poem or play or novel may be more clearly and
sharply seen. In accordance with this series' declared aim, I
have tried to be objective: but I fear that this will often have
resulted in just the sort of vaguely respectful yet uninvolved
appraisal which Goethe ironically acknowledges in the above-
quoted maxim. 'Panoramic ability' is as good an epigrammatic
summing-up as any of Goethe's talent and the Goethean
œuvre. But Goethe did not write an *œuvre* for students to be
guided through—unless this be the case with some of the more
elaborate mystifications of his old age, such as the Second Part
of *Faust*. He wrote poems and plays and novels, a large number
of individual works, each demanding a particular response
from the reader; and as he was a poet, he wrote to touch, to
move, to please. His life and works appear to us as a composite

fact of intellectual history occurring at a particularly critical moment in the development of western European society, and demand to be objectively approached, studied and understood as such. Moreover, the appreciation of any individual work of complexity or profundity—even a 'pure' lyric poem, and particularly a lyric poem in a foreign language—itself demands in the first instance uncommitted, objective understanding, a detached effort of the mind. But it is a failure of aesthetic response if the reader does not make some attempt to decide which of the works he likes best, which of them touch him, move him and please him the most. Therefore in conclusion I offer a few more personal judgements.

Goethe was and remained first and foremost a lyric poet. Even in lyric poetry there are certain fixed external forms which the poet may, if he chooses, adopt—loosely fixed like the ballad, firmly like the sonnet or the classical elegiac distich; but broadly speaking, the lyric poet creates his own forms. Each new content, each new vision or experience, demands the creation of a new form to fit it. Even where the fixed forms are used successfully, this is really little more than a fortunate coincidence, as when Goethe sees that the shape of a particular emotional experience will happily fit that of a sequence of sonnets. Goethe was primarily a creator of forms, and therefore primarily a lyric poet. Every phase of his life produced great lyric poetry, even though in the works of each phase one finds different qualities to admire. The 'Sturm und Drang' poetry one remembers and treasures for its immediacy and vigour. In the early Weimar years these qualities are to some extent lost, even deliberately suppressed, and at times the poetry suffers, but the best of it—the verses for Charlotte von Stein—has its own characteristic excellence, a mysterious sense of imperilled calm. The confidence and poised strength of the classical poetry present a complete contrast, and strange though it may seem to find a northern European poet in the last decades of the eighteenth century deliberately imitating antique metres and styles, in the *Römische Elegien* and *Hermann und Dorothea* this rises far beyond mere literary affectation. The late poetry is quite different again. The best of this presents a new kind of mystery and a new kind of serenity, and is perhaps the 'purest' of all Goethe's poetry, in the sense of language purified as with a refiner's fire.

Goethe was greater as a poet than as a novelist, and I think greater, generally speaking, as a novelist than as a dramatist, though with the qualification that some of his verse plays excel by reason of their poetry. Like the lyric poet, the novelist creates his own forms: the elaborate distinctions and classifications of modern critics of fiction cannot ultimately bring us past this simple fact. Triumphantly in *Werther*, more dubiously but still impressively in *Wilhelm Meisters Lehrjahre*, Goethe allows the experience and the vision to create their own appropriate form. *Die Wahlverwandtschaften* is regarded by many critics as his greatest novel; but reading and re-reading it I find it hard to resist the impression of a too conscious, wilful manipulation of form, and of an attempt to make the novel carry more than this particular novel can. Still more puzzling is the *Wanderjahre*, where wilful manipulation of form is combined, if that is the right word, with wilful disregard of it. To me *Die Wahlverwandtschaften* and the *Wanderjahre* suggest that Goethe might better in this period of his life have chosen to write within the confines of the self-contained 'Novelle' or short story, thereby achieving a concentration and economy similar to that of the late lyric poetry and leaving the thematic connexions and reflexions to take care of themselves.

In the writing of plays, the poet whose natural bent is to the continuous creation of new forms is placed at something of a disadvantage by the physical circumstances of dramatic performance and the existence of well-established traditional forms particularly adapted to these circumstances. Certain ways of writing plays for stage performance have for long and with good reason been regarded as more likely to succeed than others. This is not to say that it is impossible for the play-wright to ignore these forms and create his own. It is compromise which is perhaps more dangerous. Thus Goethe's most success-ful dramatic work seems to me to be *Tasso*, precisely that work which is furthest from the traditional forms of tragedy and comedy and furthest from arousing the traditional expectations associated with them—though the persistence of these expecta-tions, ingrained in generations of theatre-goers and dramatic critics, still leads to misinterpretation of the play. *Tasso* simply exhibits a situation of endemic conflict without coming to that resolution of conflict which drama traditionally seeks to present, without even—and this is more important—seriously implying at any point that the conflict will be decisively resolved in the traditional way. *Egmont* and *Iphigenie*, on the other hand, do, I think, arouse but ultimately fail to satisfy traditional expec-tations associated with the notion of tragedy. Similarly amongst the minor plays *Stella* seems to me greatly superior to *Clavigo* because, for all the superficial ease with which it can be adapted to the traditional demands of tragedy, it does not seriously arouse them, but essentially works all the time towards the original open, conciliatory ending; whereas *Clavigo* remains throughout within the conventional limits of domestic melo-drama. In conventional dramatic terms *Götz* works as well as any of the plays, and it has the characteristic vigour of the 'Sturm und Drang', the same huge, disordered vitality as Schiller's *Räuber*.

With the exception of the Gretchen tragedy, which is, uniquely, both, *Faust* is poetry and not drama. It exhibits on an enormous scale the fault which on a smaller scale mars Marlowe's *Doctor Faustus* and is indeed probably inseparable from any attempted dramatic treatment of the legend. In Aristotelian terms, it has a beginning and an end but no middle: what comes between the pact and its ultimate resolution creates no dramatic movement. It is, to put it very crudely, only padding; it does, however, contain some of Goethe's greatest verse, and it is for this that one returns to *Faust* rather than for drama or for any sense of formal totality.

Of Goethe the sage I shall say nothing. His wisdom is a poet's wisdom and cannot be isolated from his poetry, though some may feel that the wisdom of poets would make the world wiser. Each phase of his work has its treasures to reveal, and at each re-reading one finds oneself remembering former pleasures and discovering new ones, changing one's preferences, sometimes even being unmoved by things which had previously excited one, yet knowing that on some future visit the old magic will be reawakened. It is in this confidence of inexhaustible poetic riches that one acknowledges Goethe's place among the great.

Bibliography

Editions

These are innumerable, but two are deserving of special mention.

1. The 'Hamburger Ausgabe': *Goethes Werke*, ed. Erich Trunz and others, Hamburg (Christian Wegner Verlag), first published 1948, now in its eighth printing: 14 vols. plus index and 6 vols. of correspondence. The *HA* is far from complete, including for example only a selection of the poems, only the definitive versions of major works and a selection of the minor dramas, scientific works, etc. But it is indispensable for its very full, helpful and provocative notes, and its extensive bibliographies, which are kept well up to date.

2. The 'dtv' paperback edition: *Goethe: Sämtliche Werke*, ed. Peter Boerner and others, 45 vols., dtv (= Deutscher Taschenbuch-Verlag), based on the texts of the Artemis edition: inexpensive, attractively printed, reliable, the best working texts for the student.

Mention should also be made of David Luke's admirable selection of Goethe's poetry in the 'Penguin Poets' series, with an introduction and plain prose translations as well as the German text.

Biography and criticism

The following works in English are particularly useful:

1. G. H. Lewes, *The Life and Works of Goethe*. First published in 1855, frequently reprinted (Everyman's Library): still the best biography, and a classic in its own right.

2. R. Friedenthal, *Goethe, his life and times*, London 1965 (originally published in German). The fullest modern biography. Controversial.

3. Barker Fairley, *A Study of Goethe*, Oxford 1969 (second edition). The best general critical study in English. The same author's *Goethe's Faust. Six Essays* (Oxford 1953) is also worthy of special recommendation.

4. E. M. Wilkinson and L. A. Willoughby, *Goethe, Poet and Thinker*, London 1962. A collection of stimulating critical essays on a variety of topics.

5. R. Peacock, *Goethe's Major Plays*, Manchester 1959. Critical.

6. E. C. Mason, *Goethe's Faust, its Genesis and Purport*, California 1967. Critical, with extensive discussion of the work of earlier scholars, and bibliography.

7. H. S. Reiss, *Goethe's Novels*, London 1969. Full and valuable bibliography.

8. Wolfgang Leppmann, *The German Image of Goethe*, Oxford 1961. A history of the changing tastes and methods of Goethe criticism.

There are also valuable chapters on Goethe in:

Erich Heller, *The Disinherited Mind*, Cambridge, 1952, on 'Goethe and the Idea of Scientific Truth' and 'Goethe and the Avoidance of Tragedy'.

E. A. Blackall, *The Emergence of German as a Literary Language*, Cambridge, 1959, on the language of Goethe's early works.

The Era of Goethe. Essays presented to James Boyd, Oxford 1959.

The best introduction to German Goethe criticism for the student is provided by the *HA* (see above). The notes contain extensive quotation and paraphrase of critics other than the editors themselves.